LOOKING
for LOVE

He's Looking for You

JO ANNE RODDAM

outskirts
press™

Outskirts Press, Inc.
http://www.outskirtspress.com

Paperback ISBN: 978-1-9772-2115-5
Hardback ISBN: 978-1-9772-2116-2

Outskirts Press and the "OP" logo are trademarks belonging to Outskirts Press, Inc.

PRINTED IN THE UNITED STATES OF AMERICA

Gratefully dedicated to the Bridge Club's current members: Ann Byers, Sandra Barnett, Sandy Wheeler Brothers, Susan Huff, Marcia Miller, Mary Carolyn Sullivan and Joel Thompson and past members Pam Collier, Jean Colquitt, Judy Gilbert, Betty Harrison and Neal Haskew. Also dedicated to my friend and hair stylist, Jo Anne Humber.

This group of ladies has been instrumental in shaping my Christian growth by their actions, their talk, and their gentle correction. I learned from them how to respond to my husband, how to raise my children and how to cook many of their delicious recipes. They don't gossip; they talk and laugh about themselves.

For 40+ years we've had the club, I've appreciated them praying for me and my family as they have for each other, for the needs of Christians and for the world. They've discussed the Bible, how to apply God's word to our lives and held each other accountable to be good witnesses for the Lord.

I have wonderful memories of out-of-town trips with them over the years. But it was the monthly fellowship with them that helped me grow in my Christian walk. Thank you all.

But most of all it is dedicated to the Roy who loved me, taught me, and just put up with me for over 50 years, and to our three children by birth, Roy Jr., Renee and Randy, our two children by marriage, Hope Roddam and Derek Richesin and five blessings, called grandchildren: Reid Richesin, Ross Richesin, Jane Anne Roddam, Julia Roddam and John Roddam.

But it was all made possible by the love and grace of our Lord and Savior.

2020

Table of Contents

Chapter 1

I'D BEEN SEARCHING for a husband for years. If I could find just the right man, that would be the solution to my loneliness.

Love is all I had ever wanted. Throughout my childhood I knew I had my father's love but I was unsure of Mother's.

After pleading for years for a husband, God had finally given me the best gift - this husband. I prayed for children and again, I got better than I deserved. My lifelong goal, to be married and have children, was reached. I thought it would make me happy. But it didn't. My self doubt continued to make me miserable.

I wondered why my husband married me. We only have sex in common. There has to be more to a relationship than just that, but that is when I am a part of his life.

I'm not a part of his world of medicine. I can't play his main recreational activity, golf, because at home I have no help with our three preschool children.

But it is just me. I want to be sure of his love. I want him to meet my needs without my having to tell him.

I can understand. I don't look enticing when he gets home. I'm too tired to care ... tired of refereeing arguments between three little combatants, tired of cleaning and re-cleaning without any visual evidence and physically tired of never having any time off from this life I chose.

And I chose it. It was all I ever wanted ... to impress the world with what I had caught and what we had produced. I hit the jackpot.

But nothing changed. Nothing is going to change, except that I could make my children unhappy, like me. I didn't know how to be a good mother.

The children needed to be in church. I needed to be there too. My father, who I knew loved me, had recently died. I hoped it would help me manage them and my depression. So I took the children to one nearby and went with them to their Sunday School class. Soon after Roy gave up his Sunday golf game and started attending church with us. Now I had him to go with me to the adult Sunday school class.

One weekend the church had a Lay Witness Weekend, where out-of-town people gave their testimonies. They had something I wanted - peace.

We broke into little groups and the out-of-town woman in my group asked me, "Jo Anne, how do you expect to get into heaven?"

How dare she ask me that question in public. That was the reason I was going to church to find out how to get to heaven. Daddy was so good he had to be there. I wanted to see him again so I needed to know the entrance requirements. But I had to give her some answer.

"I guess it's by keeping the Ten Commandments."

"No," she gasped, "It's by faith."

Giving the wrong answer embarrassed me. It made me angry. I knew one Bible verse, so I countered with, "What about faith without works is dead?"

"I don't know," she said, "but I know it's by faith alone."

You never get anything unless you work for it, I thought. *She doesn't know any more than I do. I'll look in the Bible's index to find out how to get to heaven."*

A patient had recently given us a Living Bible, a translation that I could understand. But there wasn't any Table of Contents, telling me where to look. God used those events to make me determined to find out the entrance requirements for heaven.

At home life among the little savages continued as I increasingly got more depressed. I knew I wasn't a good mother. I feared our children would turn out like me, instead of being like their father.

What chance would my children have to come out 'normal' under my care?

I knew I wouldn't be absent from my children's lives, like my own mother had been. Because she worked she was never available, so I felt I wasn't important to her. Maybe it would have been better if I had worked outside the home because I knew I wasn't as loving and supportive as my Dad had always been.

Although I loved Roy, I resented that his life was still his own. He did as he wanted. But I no longer did anything except caring for them.

I started each day planning to be different, but soon my resentment and self pity built up, until it bubbled over into sarcasm, screams, threats and even spankings. The children were messy, fussy, angry, selfish and lazy. They were just like me. We become like the people we are around and they were only around me. Roy left early for work and arrived back home after they were fed and ready for bed, so he had little time to be with them. I wouldn't ask for help and I couldn't just walk away. But, I couldn't stay either. I loved them too much to jeopardize their future. It would be better for them if I was no longer around. Somebody else could do a better job.

Isolation kills you - knowing you are alone. I wished I had someone to talk to, to advise me, to tell me what to do. *Is there anyone who feels like I do? How could I tell others about being a bad mother?* I didn't dare let anyone know what went on at our house or how I felt, so I built a wall of silence to keep everyone out. There was just no one with whom I could open up. It really didn't seem worth the effort.

I felt I couldn't even talk to Roy. He had a lot of pressure on him in his new job at the Baptist Hospitals, where he was trying to establish an Internal Medicine residency program. When he told me about his difficulties, I couldn't add to them. I didn't say anything about the thoughts I was having. Deep down I was afraid if I complained he might leave me. I felt so unsure of his love that I didn't want to do anything to upset him. He seemed oblivious to any of my problems, not knowing how much I needed him. I had no time or place of escape. I wanted out.

April 22nd was the day I finally gave up and decided to end it all. There was no use putting it off.

I can't take it any longer. It won't get any better. It never does.

Roy's father, a city bus driver, would get home around 3 p.m. I would use some pretense to get him to keep the children. Then I would return to our house, pull in the garage, close the garage door and just leave the car running until I went to sleep - forever. The odorless gas would end my misery.

Roy would mourn me for awhile but he can easily find another wife. The children are so young they won't even remember me very long. It certainly will be better for them. No one will miss me. Even my mother didn't want to be around me. She worked to escape being home with me. She didn't want me; she must think I'm ugly. Then when I finally met my "prince" and got him to marry me, he learned what the other guys knew - something was wrong with me. It seemed to me that Roy, like my mother, was home as little as possible. And when he was home, to distance himself from me, he shut his office door as if he was closing me out of his world.

As I sat thinking this and planning my suicide, the phone rang. Susan Huff, an acquaintance from church, called to invite me to a Bible study, share group. I hated activities like that. Besides I wouldn't be around to attend. I made some excuse but she must have heard the sadness in my voice because before she hung up she said, "Jo Anne, God loves you and I love you."

The tears started rolling down my cheeks and it was all I could do to get off the phone before she realized I was crying. You may never know how doing a small, seemingly unimportant job, like calling a list of people, can really make an impact on someone's life. But it didn't change my plan.

While I waited for my father-in-law to get home from work, I got the mail. In it was a Baptist publication. We were not Baptists and had never been. It was not addressed to anyone who had ever lived in our house. It was intended for a home clearly across Birmingham, Al. on Avenue Q in the Pratt City area, a long way from our home in Vestavia. There was no reason for it to be in our mailbox. On the cover of the pamphlet was a box-in area that said, "To Be or Not To Be, See Page Four". I sat down at the kitchen table, turned to the fourth page and read the article entitled, "Why God Doesn't Want You To Commit Suicide".

In amazement I realized that God, who created everything, had sent me a "letter" about suicide. Most of the points in the sermon by the West End Baptist pastor, I knew well because they described me. Rev. Louis Wilhite wrote that one cause of suicide is reaching the goal you have worked for and then realizing it is not what you expected. He was so right. What I had always wanted, being a wife and mother, amounted to nothing since I felt I had failed. Like he said, suicidal people have no plans for the future. I couldn't see myself ever succeeding. I only saw tragedy ahead.

Rev. Wilhite said we fail to teach our children that we love them, just for being and not for anything that they do. I tried all my life to win my mother's acceptance.

Most people who have lost hope will tell you about how they were mistreated. I was angry about some things in the past but I was mainly angry at myself, anger turned inward. Because I couldn't love myself, I felt no one could really love me. As Rev. Wilhite said, I felt I had no real friends. If they knew me they wouldn't like me.

"But we only need one person to love us," the pastor said, "and if you think you have no one to love you, you are wrong. You have God."

There really is a God. How amazing. He acted in my life by causing Susan to call me and tell me that He loves me. He demonstrated that love by having a Baptist pastor write that article and then by putting it in my mailbox, today. Those were not coincidences. God ... I'm going to find out about you.

I called Susan back and told her I wanted to attend her Bible study. Years later I leaned that the woman, who had asked me how I expected to get to heaven, had been staying with Susan. She told Susan there was one person she was going to be praying for - me.

At the Bible study I learned that Christ fulfilled all the Old Testament prophecies about the coming Messiah. I was so excited about what I was learning that Roy wanted to go to a study for couples. There was one not far from our home.

Every week Mabel and John Donaldson emptied their living-dining room combination of all the furniture except the couch and chairs, which they pushed against the walls. The dining room table was moved to the den and held refreshments. Also weekly their son, John Jr., borrowed a truck load of folding chairs from Briarwood Presbyterian Church for rows of seats and then returned them after the meeting. Mabel used the name tags, kept for the next week, to pray for those attending.

We didn't know the Donaldsons, anyone attending, the location of any of the books in the Bible or the preacher teaching. We went anyway and were amazed at this humble pastor who really believed what he taught. He told stories of how exactly his prayers were answered at the last minute without anyone knowing of his need. Soon we got a standing baby sitter and continued going to that Bible study for years and years.

There Rev. Frank Barker Jr. explained you couldn't earn and didn't deserve your salvation because if you wanted to go to heaven based on how you lived, you had to have a perfect record with no sins. All have sinned so the only way you can get in is if someone with that perfect obedience gives you his record. Jesus was sinless. You have to ask Him to be your Savior and your Lord, then He gives you his perfect record. I wanted Him to save me and make me a better person. That's when I became a Christian. Accepting that He died for you as your Savior is easy but letting Him be your Lord and rule your life is a daily, lifetime battle.

I knew from early childhood, that God was watching me. I remembered standing on a chair, so I could reach the salt which I had poured out on the table. Then, I licked my finger so the salt would stick to it. I had an unusual love of salt, probably because it was my 'forbidden fruit'. I'd been told not to eat salt; too much was bad for you. What you can't have, you always want, so I disobeyed just like Eve did in the Garden of Eden.

A neighbor, Hutchie, short for Mrs. Hutchinson, kept me while my parents worked. Hearing her sewing machine, I knew she was busy so I could eat all the salt I wanted and she wouldn't know. Then, I remembered she told me there was someone who saw everything.

"Forgive me, Lord Jesus," I said as I continued to dip my finger in the salt and lick it off. "I know this is wrong but it is so-o-o good."

It was 1944 and I was four years old. God had me remember this as my earliest memory to show me what a hypocrite I was from the very beginning - acknowledging my sin, asking for forgiveness, but then continuing the very action I just confessed.

God Is active in the life of every believer. Although many may not recognize this, some know it was His hand that controlled events in their life.

A friend, Carolyn Crowe, told of trying to bargain with God for the life of her third daughter, Julie, who had a severe heart problem.

"If you will just heal her, I will live 100% for you," she promised after a particularly bad time. That was a turning point because Carolyn said although she was living for God, she had not been giving Him her whole heart.

Her daughter, Julie, almost six, was on digitalis. Dr. John Kirklin, a world-renowned heart surgeon, gave her only a 40% chance of surviving the surgery to remove a growing, benign tumor.

"During my quiet time with the Lord," Carolyn remembers, "God spoke to me so clearly that it almost seemed verbal, 'Okay, I'm going to give you one more week with Julie. After that, she is going to be with Me.' I didn't tell anyone but on the day of surgery I sensed she was on her way to be with God.

"Although Julie's death was a tragedy, it was God's plan. When you have a deep-rooted, unshakable confidence that God loves you and is in control of every situation, the tragedies in life lose their sting." Carolyn said. "That doesn't mean that I did not grieve, but it means I did not despair."

Later a second daughter, Melanie, as a young adult needed heart surgery to repair a hole in her heart and to correctly connect the main heart artery.

The morning of her surgery, as Carolyn awaited the second heart surgery on a daughter, she was encouraged as she read Isaiah 65:20-24. The 23rd verse said, "They will not toil in vain or bear children doomed to misfortune; for they will be a people blessed by the Lord, they and their descendants after them."

These verses seemed to tell Carolyn that Melanie would recover from this operation and would have children. "It was just like God spoke to me, as He had before Julie died." Melanie carried a copy of these verses into the operating room with her. The surgery was a success.

"That's how we had two daughters that went through heart surgery, one that was successful and one that was not," Carolyn said. "But God was faithful in both outcomes and His plan was accomplished."

So Carolyn and I both saw the Lord do amazing things in our lives.

Chapter 2

HUTCHIE NEVER HEARD me misbehaving. Maybe she couldn't hear because she was so old. Living on a direct approach to the nearby airport you couldn't hear anything, when the planes passed directly overhead, because they were so loud. Lots of military airplanes flew over during the war years, on their way to be repaired at the airfield. But you couldn't always talk when they weren't passing over. We shared our one telephone with another family on a "party line" which meant we could only use the phone when they were not talking on it. You never had to look for the phone. It was always in the same place, where it was connected by a wire, which ran outside to the telephone line.

Hutchie's house was on the corner and our house was right in the middle of the nine houses on our block on Fourth Avenue North, between 79th and 80th Streets in the East Lake section of Birmingham. Like the other clapboard houses, ours was two rooms wide with a living room, dining room, kitchen, bathroom, two and a half bedrooms and a large front porch.

Our house was big enough for my parents, me, and Robert, my brother, who was seven years older than me. My parents slept in one double bed; my brother slept in another. And I had a twin bed which filled most of my tiny room. But soon five relatives came to board with us and share our three beds. As our family got up, the boarders, who worked nights, were coming to get into our beds. It was a winning situation for all. They had a place to live, while they worked modifying B-24 and B-20 bombers to help with the war effort. Their rent gave us extra money and ration stamps, which were necessary to buy many items like sugar, meat, tires and gasoline.

While Daddy packed lunches Mama cooked breakfast. Most mornings the aroma of frying bacon, scrambled eggs, grits and biscuits woke me before Mama called. As with all our meals you ate what was put before you or you didn't eat. That being the only choice, you developed a taste for everything. There were no picky eaters. We all ate together at the same time and at the kitchen table, not all over the house.

With the renters now in our beds, the family and a few extra paying riders packed our black, '38 Dodge sedan to go to work after dropping me off at Hutchie's. Some got out at the airfield factory jobs and others were picked up to ride the rest of the way downtown. My parents looked for ways to earn extra money. Daddy was an artist for the Birmingham News and did freelance art work at home on Saturdays and Sundays. This interfered with his attending church but he encouraged the rest of us to go.

Mama's parents had been sharecroppers with nine children to feed. Daddy was raised hungry along with his other seven siblings. His absentee father, a tile setter who lived in Birmingham, only returned occasionally to his family out in the country. The 'old man,' as he was called, expected his wife to raise enough to feed their family. But she rarely could provide enough food and they frequently went to bed hungry.

With their background my parents were determined to give my brother and me a better life. Mother also worked in the art department at the News until the men returned after serving overseas during World War II. We raised chickens and grew our vegetables in the large Victory Garden behind our house.

Most Easters I got two baby chickens, dyed pink or purple. I raised them in a box until they could get out. Then, they had to join the other chickens in the backyard. I never liked eating chicken. It might be one of my pets. It would be like eating your dog.

Christmas was the big holiday. Daddy cut a cedar tree in the woods. Big multicolored lights, sometimes with metal reflectors around them, made the tree look on fire - a real concern as the tree dried out. Strings of multicolored, glass beads were strung as garlands around the glass ornaments. An angel topped the tree and strips of silver, foil icicles were hung or thrown on the tree. Our packages were wrapped in thin, white tissue paper with coiling ribbon and Christmas stickers. Mistletoe was shot down from a tree and hung so that anyone caught under it, got a kiss. That was all our decorations.

I usually got a few little things and one big present, often a doll. The last one was a Toni doll when I was 13; the year before I got a skating doll. Both of those survived because I was outgrowing those toys. An electric blanket was one of my favorite gifts. Then I could have a warm bed without the weight of all those quilts. I thought it was heaven.

We didn't have heat vents in each room, just a pot belly stove which was later replaced by a floor furnace. That and a fireplace kept us warm but away from those it was nippy. Summers were hot. The feel good times were fall and spring.

"I don't want to go to Hutchie's. I want to stay home with you. Do I have to go?"

Mother stopped brushing her hair, "Someone has to keep you while I work."

"Why do you have to work? Don't you want to be with me?"

"Of course, I do," Mama said. "But we need the money so you and Robert can go to college. When you are older you will understand. Don't you like to stay with Hutchie?"

"I like Hutchie. I just miss you, I want to be with you."

"Soon you will start school and have lots of friends so you won't have to stay there much longer."

With the end of the war the relatives left, the servicemen returned,

my mother found another job and I started Barrett Elementary School. Robert, almost a teenager, could watch me after school ... not that he wanted a little sister interfering in his life.

"Get out of the way," Robert yelled at me. "We're trying to play football."

"Let me play."

"You are too little. You'd get hurt. Who ever heard of a girl playing football. Go play with your dolls. Because of you, we have to have our games here."

The neighborhood boys met and played in our front yard. It was relatively flat and their game could spill out across the sidewalk into the usually deserted street. The other boys didn't have to tend to any younger siblings; their mothers were at home. In fact, our mother was the only one in the neighborhood who worked.

Robert delighted in tormenting me. "You're adopted. You don't really belong in our family." Or he would tell me, "Mama and Daddy aren't coming back."

But the worst allegations were that I had ancestors and even garments on me. I thought those must be as bad as having cooties, which all the school children accused each other of having. One thing I knew, someday I would grow big enough to beat him up. I dreamed of the day I would get even. That was the beginning of my way of dealing with enemies.

Hutchie and her husband moved to a farm in south Georgia when I was 10. A couple of times I rode alone on the train to visit them. The conductor watched out for me; I was perfectly safe. For years as a child, I rode the streetcar and later the bus downtown alone. I got off at First Avenue and walked four blocks to the Birmingham News building. Although very young, I was safe on those trips. Kidnappings of ordinary children were unknown.

Hutchie had told me we have guardian angels watching over us. She didn't know how right she was. I never knew the term, pervert, until I was grown. But I experienced one. The father of a neighborhood friend made a 'swing' by joining his hands to form a 'seat'. But

when he swung me he put his fingers inside my panties. I didn't know what he was doing but I knew it was wrong. And I knew enough to avoid ever being alone with him. I was too ashamed to tell my parents. I thank God that I was protected from that neighbor and any others as I traveled on buses, trains and walked to and from school by myself.

The sidewalk lining our street was our highway to the world. As children we walked, roller skated, or rode our bikes everywhere on the sidewalk to explore. It was perfect for hop scotch or jump rope. And on hot summer evenings families walked up and down the street, stopping to visit at different homes. I loved sitting on our porch swing with my Dad as the adults, sitting on the glider, laughed and recounted tales from their past. But soon the lure of the children catching lightening bugs, playing hide 'n seek or farmer in the dell, drew me outside our screened porch.

"Bedtime. Bedtime." It seemed too soon to face my stifling bedroom. All our beds were pushed against the windowsills to try to feel a cool, night breeze. We didn't even have a fan to move the air.

On the long summer nights when Daddy wasn't doing advertising art jobs, he illustrated and wrote several serial feature articles which he sold for years to newspapers across the U.S. To everybody he was just Johnny. I knew he loved me.

He was getting bald and had the beginning of a protrusion which would enlarge to a real belly with age but I loved his heart. He was kind to everyone and reached out to those in need, sharing the little bit we had and giving encouragement. I thought he was wonderful. I don't remember him cursing and rarely saw him angry. I thought he could do anything, make anything or try anything. He encouraged me to do the same.

His light blue eyes would twinkle as he told me, "You can do it. Go on and try. You learn by doing and you'll get better with each attempt."

Neither Daddy or I knew at that time that all our practice is to no avail unless the Lord allows it to result in success. Ultimately God is

the one who gives us all our abilities. Not giving God the credit and feeling that we have done it ourselves is pride. God hates the proud heart and we are warned that pride goes before destruction. I later learned that everything we have was given to us by God.

Sometimes in winter, when it was too cold to sit outside, Daddy would read aloud to us. I would sit on his lap as we gathered in front of the fireplace in the living room.

I remember as he read scary scenes from "The Wizard of Oz" I buried my face into his chest and screamed, "Stop. Stop. Don't read anymore."

"It's just make believe, Monkey," he told me. "Dorothy will get through this. She has someone looking out for her."

Someone was looking out for a friend, Dean Hodge, and her husband when they were in a plane crash. Her husband, Glenn, was not a Christian and Dean had been praying for Glenn to believe and commit to following Christ. He loved to fly their small, private airplane. On one trip the gas gage registered, full. But as they were flying the plane began to sputter and Glenn realized it was out of gas. In the heavily wooded area there was no open space to land. Dean silently prayed as they prepared to crash, "Please save us so Glenn won't die as a non-believer."

God answered that prayer and they both walked away from their totaled airplane. But the bigger miracle was Glenn recognized how close he came to being separated forever from God and Dean. He asked Christ to save him for eternity.

Besides books, we had to imagine the characters and scenes, as we listened to our favorite shows on our floor model radio. But I didn't need pictures to visualize some speakers such as the Lone Ranger,

Roy Rogers or the Cisco Kid. We saw them on Saturdays when children got in for a dime at the movie theatre. We could spend all day watching, over and over, a cowboy or Tarzan movie, a cartoon and news reels.

At night families viewed films from their cars on the big screen at drive-in movies. Dressed in pajamas, children were ready to be carried in and put to bed when they returned home. The rise of television began the demise of going to the movie theaters and drive-ins.

We got the first TV on our block. Neighbors came to see the novelty and no one argued about what show to watch on either of the two black and white channels, on until midnight. Until we got a television we didn't know how poor we were. We lived just like everybody else in our neighborhood. The TV showed us the homes, cars and possessions of others.

"Mama, Mama. I'm singing a solo at school next Friday. Will you come?"

She closed the drawer after putting away the folded underwear. "Oh I would love to see you perform but you know I can't. I have to work."

"But Mama this is special. My class is putting on this show for all the parents and the rest of the school. Everyone else's mother will be there."

"Jo Anne, you know I'm working then. I can't take off from work for just any little old thing."

"Couldn't you come just this once." I crossed my fingers for good luck, hoping this time she would ask off.

"I can't, Jo Anne. I might lose my job. You'll do fine."

How do you know, I thought. *You've never been to anything I was in. You have time to do what you wants to do. You have time to do things with Robert. You just likes him better. You don't like girls. Are you ashamed of me? Do you even love me?*

Mother kept her trim shape by daily exercise and hard work in the garden. She loved her dark hair and pulled out the gray hairs as they first appeared. Later she dyed her hair to keep it black. She told me, "Hair turns really dark just in time for the gray to show up."

Once I asked her, "Did you ever think about having a little girl?"

"I suppose I did."

"What did you think she would be like?"

"I pictured her with beautiful brown eyes and dark hair," she told me.

I must have been a disappointment. I took after my Dad with blue eyes and blond hair. I sure wished I had dark hair or at least brown eyes.

It wasn't that Mother was cruel. She just didn't think how that would hurt me.

Mothers love their children. They don't intentionally say things to hurt them. But words can be misunderstood and plant seeds that harvest a lifetime of tears. My whole life I felt I wasn't quite good enough. I just didn't measure up. Apparently she didn't even care what I was named so she let my seven-year-old brother name me for his girl friend in his second grade class.

"Why did you let Robert name me?" I asked mother as she sat folding the clothes she had just taken off the clothes line.

"I didn't have any girl's names picked out," she answered. "I didn't think I would have a girl."

"Why was that? Didn't you want a little girl?"

"Well, I guess I never wanted a girl." She saw the look on my face. "Oh, but I'm glad I have you. You're my buddy," she said as she gave me a hug.

But I was thinking, *Mama didn't want me.* "Why didn't you want a girl?" I asked.

"Because life is so hard for a woman."

Chapter 3

DADDY TOOK ONE of the hot biscuits and flipped it with his thumb so it rolled across the top of the chrome trimmed, red, metal kitchen table. About an inch in circumference, the small, hard balls did resemble marbles more than biscuits. As the tears began to spill down my cheeks, I grabbed the plate of biscuit-balls and threw them in the sink.

His laughter ceased as he saw my pain. "I'm sorry, honey," he said as he put his arm around me. "They are really cooked just as I like them." He went and retrieved the biscuits.

"Forgive me for making fun of your cooking. You are actually doing a good job. Soon, you'll be as good a cook as your mother." To prove it he popped a biscuit in his mouth, but I could see he had to struggle to chew it.

To teach me how to cook and to help Mother with the evening meals, she and I would plan dinner and do some of the preparations before she left for her job. She worked at the Atlantic and Pacific warehouse checking to see that the eggs were good and not fertilized before they were sold in the A & P grocery stores. After my high school classes I would finish cooking so that dinner was ready when my parents got home from work. That morning I had made a Jello and fruit salad and brought the dried black-eyed peas to a boil, leaving them to soak the rest of the day. Fried pork chops, cooked cabbage and my biscuits completed the menu.

I had made biscuits in my 8th grade home economics class at

elementary school but that was under close supervision. These resembled the little mud balls I used to make for my doll family in my backyard playhouse. Daddy built it for me when I was about nine. It was furnished with a little girl size rocking chair, stove, refrigerator, and an high chair and iron doll bed. My prized possession was a table and chairs which Daddy had made and beautifully painted with hearts and flowers. I played there many hours taking care of my dolls. I bathed them, dressed them, "cooked" grass, leaves and acorns for them and cleaned my little house while they slept.

It seemed a lot of those early years were preparation to be a wife and mother. I liked cooking and I didn't even mind cleaning. I knew I was going to be a stay-at-home mom. No career for me. I'd be at home when my children got home from school. I'd attend all their performances and school functions. I'd even join the P.T. A.

And if I had a daughter I would tell her how glad I was to have her. I would make sure she knew I loved her.

I was happy in elementary school and looked forward to going to Woodlawn High School. But during my 8th grade year we moved across town to Mt. Brook. I was allowed to finish the year with my friends at Barrett by riding one bus, and then transferring to another, to reach my school in East Lake. After graduation I had to enroll at the nearby Shades Valley High School.

Five or six elementary schools funneled their graduates to the only high school over Red Mountain. The teens from rich families in Mt. Brook, Vestavia, and Homewood outnumbered the poorer students, bused in from the county's rural areas. It seemed I didn't fit in either group. Most of the ninth graders had their own friends from their grammar school. I was alone. I didn't know a soul.

"What's your name?" the girl sitting in the desk in front of me in homeroom asked. "It's Jo Anne, isn't it?"

"Yes. Jo Anne Padgett."

"Where did you go to elementary school?"

"Barrett."

"I never heard of it. Where's that?"

"It's in East Lake."

"East Lake," she repeated as she sort of curled up her nose. She thought for a minute and said, "Well, what sororities are rushing you, Jo Anne?"

"Sororities," I paused. "None, I guess; I don't know what sororities are."

"You don't?" she said with a smirk. "I guess they don't have sororities in East Lake."

Welcome to Shades Valley High School.

I begged to go to Woodlawn but my parents wouldn't let me. "Nobody talks to me. They all talk to their friends. I hate it. I'm miserable. Please let me go to Woodlawn."

They insisted I would make friends and wouldn't let me transfer. I was alone in homeroom and in my classes. I tried not to draw attention to myself, never asking or answering questions. I may have seemed shy, quite or reserved but I was filled with hate. In the halls I got behind the tallest person and followed as closely as I could, trying to hide as we changed classes. I made good grades. I had nothing else to do.

Even by the third year I still didn't fit in.

"I hate everyday I have to go to school. The poorer kids are called 'red necks'. When they make snide remarks about those from the country, it is just like they are making fun of you. I hate school just like you did."

Mother shook her head, "Girls can be so cruel. Don't pay any attention. You have nice clothes and you are just as good as they are."

"I know but I'm so unhappy. They are like the ones who laughed because you had only two dresses to wear to high school."

The pain I felt made me angry with myself as well as them. My parents and grandparents were poor people so I identified with the ones they ridiculed.

Malcolm Forbes, former publisher of Forbes Magazine, said, "You can easily judge the character of others by how they treat those who they think can do nothing for them."

Inwardly, I seethed when the snooty girls would snicker and cover their mouths with their hands, as they whispered, while their eyes watched the ones they were talking about. I hurt for the ones being singled out, but I didn't say or do anything to help them. I didn't try to befriend them; I didn't want to be part of the persecuted. I saw them talking about me, too.

I didn't know that a Harvard psychologist said that having even one child on the victim's side deters a bully. He suggested catching the bully alone, telling him to stop those actions because you don't like what he is doing and then threatening to report it if it continues. He suggested rehearsing this assertive behavior before saying it to the bully.[1]

Although I didn't know it, God said vengeance is mine. He hates those prideful ones who harass the poor and think they are so much better than others. I became increasingly more self conscious. *There must be something wrong with me. If I was pretty, smart or rich they might want to be my friend.* I wanted to be a part of the 'in' group and didn't see how two faced that made me. Yet, I regretted not telling them how insensitive and callous they were. Bullies are successful because their behavior is not challenged. Because I didn't confront them I felt unworthy of respect.

I can't stand this, I thought to myself. *I hate this school. They may forget me but I'll always remember how they hurt me and others. I'm so angry. One more year and I'll be out of Shades Valley. I will never come back. I wish I was out now. I wonder if it hurts to slit your wrists.*

I took the single edge razor blade in my right hand and sliced across my left arm.

I wasn't holding the blade in the middle so the cut was deeper in the center of the slit. It wasn't very painful. I saw the white tissue standing open and then the blood began rushing out, filling the cut and then overflowing onto the bathroom counter and then, the floor. What a mess it was making.

The slice wasn't at the wrist. I had cut up too far on my arm, missing the artery. *I couldn't even do that right,* I thought.

---

1   Elin McCoy, "Bully-Proof Your Child," Reader's Digest Nov 1992, 199-204

But I knew it was a mistake. I wouldn't let them defeat me. Later in life I realized it was God who prevented my suicide.

I'd better clean this up before Mother gets home. I'll have to find some way to keep my arm hidden.

By holding a towel on the cut and then wrapping my arm with a tight bandage, I managed to stop the bleeding. I cleaned up the blood, washed a load of clothes and put on a long sleeve shirt. My parents never knew.

When I became an adult some of those I though were so snooty became my friends. I was probably projecting a lot of my self hate as coming from them.

"Are you going to follow your brother and go to the University of Alabama?" Daddy asked as we ate dinner, sitting on the three sided, red, vinyl bench that Daddy had built around the red, metal kitchen table. Mother loved red so Daddy had painted the ceiling red too.

"It doesn't look like I'm going to get married, so I guess I'll go there."

"Get married, my foot," my mother exclaimed. "Don't be in such a hurry. Have fun while you can."

"You don't have much longer in high school," Daddy said. "What are you going to study?

"Art, I guess," I said smiling. "Then if I have to work I can probably get a job in the Art Department at the Birmingham News." Daddy, as their Art Director, did the hiring.

"If you want to study art you need to go to the Art Institute in Atlanta or Chicago. You wouldn't learn anything about art at the University. That school's art instruction is way too abstract."

Daddy, a commercial artist, whose work was all in realism, didn't think much of modern art. He was self taught but became proficient enough to start the Gulf State Correspondence Art School with some other men. He wrote and illustrated their text book on commercial art.

After my lonely, miserable years in high school I didn't want to be the unknown kid in school again. No, I wouldn't think of going out of state. At least at the University I would know a few people.

"Well, if I can't study art then I'll study home economics."

"No, that's one thing you won't study," Daddy said. "I'm not paying for something you can learn at home."

"Oh, it doesn't matter anyway. I'm just going to college to get a husband. I'll only be down there a year or so." Many people considered going to college get a husband as an acceptable goal in the 50s and 60s, but not my Dad.

Normally very jovial, I watched the heat rise from my father's neck up to his cheeks. When his face was so flushed it matched the red kitchen, he exploded. "What do you mean? I'm not sending you to the university to get a husband. I never had the chance to go to college and you act like it's not important. Your mother and I have worked night and day for you to be able to get a college degree. So pick out a major and plan to stay the whole four years, until you graduate."

"O.K. O.K. Calm down. I'll study journalism."

Even though I liked journalists and their world, I thought, *I'll show you. I'm not going to work. I'm going to school to study boys. I'll find someone before I graduate.*

When I had started high school I got a Saturday job at the Birmingham News as a copy girl or gofer. I liked the excitement that pulsated, almost audibly, close to a deadline. But the din was just the clicking of the typewriters and the Associated Press teletype, punctuated by a reporter or editor yelling, "copy" for me to take the story to the next phase of preparation. On those Saturdays I'd go to work with Daddy around eight in the morning and work until 10 p.m. when he got off. I was working 14 hours until the Board of Education found out and put a stop to those long Saturday hours. During the summers I worked full time.

The News hired many handicapped people to work in various departments. Daddy taught me, by word and by his example, to always be kind to those less fortunate. One of his close friends, a News photographer, had been burned as a child at a Halloween party. His face and hands were so terribly scarred that most people avoided him or looked away when we went to lunch. To Daddy he was just another friend.

I was banking all my newspaper salary and all my baby sitting money in order to buy a car. With additional money from my parents, I was able to buy a brand new, baby blue 1957 Ford Skyliner as I began my senior year in high school. That car got me attention. Its hard top would retract into the trunk area, making it a convertible. Yet it had the safety of a regular car when the top wasn't down. It gave me confidence to know I had something beautiful that no one else in school had - even if the top frequently refused to go up or down. With a V-8 engine of 400 horsepower, it would pass anything on the road, except a filling station. It took a tank of gas to drive from Birmingham to Montgomery, eighty miles.

A couple of years later, as I was headed back to the University of Alabama, I stopped at the Gulf station in Five Points South to have the oil changed. When I backed off the rack the oil light was still on. I pointed this out to the attendant.

"You know I just changed the oil. The light must be stuck or broken," he said.

I drove to Bessemer before the engine burned up. The attendant had failed to put the plug back in, after draining out the old oil.

Daddy refused to do anything about his negligence. I was sure they would have to pay for the car. Daddy said, "I'm not going to tell them. That young man would lose his job. Everybody makes mistakes. I'll buy you a car."

Later, as an adult, I met a lady in Sunday School who loved her car so much she refused to let it be stolen. Merle Howard had stopped for gas and left the keys in the car when she went inside to pay. Seeing a young man getting into her car, she ran screaming towards him. The criminal jumped out of her car and into his buddy's. On reaching her car Merle grabbed the pistol, that had been hidden inside, and began firing at the escaping man. God was active in saving her car. But more so when He didn't allow her to shoot anyone or even their automobile. Her story made the Birmingham News.

Chapter 4

IN 1958 AT the University of Alabama, I pledged Alpha Chi Omega sorority. I was glad to be a member of a group. Now, I would have lots of friends. I quickly grew to love my fellow AXOs. After my first year in Harris Dormitory I moved into the sorority house.

I knew how fortunate I was that my parents allowed me the added expense of being in a sorority. Daddy could never afford college. In fact as a child he struggled just to eat sometime. He told a story that showed how poor they were and how God provided food for his family when he was young.

"John, here's the last money we have, a quarter. Be very careful with it. Take these clean clothes to Mrs. Hester and be sure to get the twenty-five cents she owes me for washing and ironing them. Then go by the commissary and buy dried butter beans and as many pork chops as it will get for our supper. All I've got in the house is the ingredients to bake biscuits."

When he returned Mrs. Hester's clothes, she had company and told him she would pay his mother later. Disappointed that he didn't get paid, he felt in his pocket as he walked away and found, to his dismay, that he had lost the coin his mother had given him. Desperate to find it he retraced his steps but didn't find the quarter. Then he remembered he had been seeing dried butter beans, the very item his mother had told him to buy, laying here and there on the dirt road. Apparently, the sack holding them on the back of a wagon had a hole, which allowing them to drop out. Picking them up, he had to use his shirt to carry them home. There were too many for his pockets.

That night the Lord provided a big pot of butter beans to eat with their biscuits.

At the University of Alabama I continued working for the Birmingham News, now as the U of A correspondent. I got paid a pittance for an inch of copy, so I was always looking for more stories to submit. I took my own photographs and a couple of them made the front page.

"The Dean of Women, just called to tell us that she has heard there is going to be a pantie raid," Sydney Robinson, the sorority president, told the assembled members. "The dean said we absolutely must not toss any panties out the windows or even open them. She said to stay inside and ignore the boys."

What we ignored was the dean. We all ran to the windows as we heard the crowd of boys approaching the sorority house. I grabbed my huge Speed Graphic camera and went out on the upstairs porch to get pictures of the panties floating down.

This new college craze went on several years, ending with coed dorms and the sexual revolution of the late 60s and early 70s.

But this was a conservative time when coeds had to sign out at night with the time and location where they would be. They signed back in when they returned, before the door was locked at the curfew hour. This was all done for their protection.

Dates were on Friday or Saturday nights. A boy asked a girl to go to a movie, a party, a dance or to dinner. He came to pick her up wearing a suit or sports coat and slacks with a tie, unless it was a casual or costume party.

Girls wore dresses with high heels and for a football game, added gloves and a hat. School clothes were sweater sets with a white, detachable collar, straight skirts and penny loafers with white bobby socks. Our standard jewelry included a floating opal or mustard seed necklace, a charm bracelet, a circle pin and pearl earrings.

Coeds had to hide their suggestive bottoms under a skirt or raincoat because the University wouldn't allow women to appear in public in shorts, jeans or any other pants without a covering over them.

We dated a number of guys, learning about them so we could decide which ones to keep seeing and which ones to eliminate. We were trying to find our mates.

One night, when locked in at the Alpha Chi house, I was up late cramming for my Spanish final. I heard an explosion right outside the living room window. I ran and looked out to see an eight foot cross, burning within four feet of the wooden Kappa Kappa Gamma house next door.

Cross burnings, a symbol of intimidation, were frequently associated with the Ku Klux Klan. I ran to my room, grabbed my professional camera, put on my raincoat and headed next door.

Of course, it broke the rules to go out of the house after hours and it was 3 a.m. Even though the Kappas were yelling not to take any pictures, I photographed the cross. The next morning I put the film on the bus to Birmingham and called in the story. It made the front page with a by-line. The next day I was told to report to the Dean of Women.

"Jo Anne, what were you thinking?" Dean Sarah Healy asked me. "Why would you do such a thing?"

"It's my job. I'm the correspondent for the Birmingham News and that sure was big news."

Dean Healy frowned. "It's bad publicity for the University. Don't you know mothers won't send their daughters to the University because of you."

"Well, I'm sorry. But that's why I'm down here - to learn to report the news. I'm working on a degree in journalism. I was just doing what I'm suppose to be doing for my job and for my education."

"You have broken several rules. You are in serious trouble. You will have to appear before the Judiciary Council."

I got only light punishment - two weeks restriction. The offenders were never caught. It must have been a fraternity prank.

I carried my camera with me a lot of the time. On the way to a funeral in Birmingham with a boyfriend and another couple, we came upon a huge train derailment right beside the road. The two lane highway was congested with cars stopped and people milling around.

"Stop. Stop the car. I've got to get this story," I insisted. "I'll hurry."

I was excited and didn't want to be late for the funeral so I grabbed my big camera, my stenographer's notebook and a pen and literally ran in my high heels to the highway patrolman, sitting in his patrol car.

"I'm a correspondent for the Birmingham News. Can you tell me about this accident? Was anyone hurt? When did it happen? How much ..." I started rattling off my questions.

"What did you say you wanted, little lady?" he said in a deep, slow, southern drawl.

I didn't like his tone or his condescending attitude. I knew I looked younger than my years. *He must not think I'm a real reporter.* "I'm a newspaper correspondent ... ah ... reporter. I need to get the information about this train wreck. What can you tell me ..."

He interrupted me again. "What paper did you say you work for?"

"The Birmingham News. Look, I'm headed to a funeral in Birmingham with some friends. I want to get the facts quickly so we can be on our way. So if you wouldn't mind ..."

"Do you ever read the Birmingham News?"

What was this man doing? I just told him I was in a hurry. He won't give me a straight answer. Just gives me that silly smile. "Please, sir, I'm really pushed for time ..."

"This train wreck," he chuckled, "was all over the front page of the Birmingham News two days ago."

It was sure hard walking back to explain to my friends, waiting in the car.

College was different from high school. I had friends and I was happy. But I hadn't found a husband. Three guys wanted to marry me, but they didn't measure up to my standards. I wanted a husband but I was picky.

One I dated was when we both weren't dating anyone else. He was fun to be with. One night he asked me if I would marry him, if he wasn't Jewish. It made no difference to me. I admired the Jews, Catholics and Mormons because they were so sincere in the practice of their beliefs. So his religion wasn't the problem. But I just loved him as a friend.

I thought I had met my Prince Charming when I began to date Jeff. He could have walked off a fairy tale page with his good looks, black hair and blue eyes. Although he didn't play sports, he had an athlete's body and I was smitten from our first date. He was gorgeous. And he kept asking me out until we were not dating anyone else.

Although we'd been dating for a while, we had never discussed religion. I assumed he believed. I thought of myself as a Christian, even though I was entirely focused on myself, never acted like a Christian and didn't ever attend church.

Because he was studying geology, I said to Jeff one night, "I guess you can really see God's hand in creation in your studies."

"What?" he said smiling "Surely you don't believe in God."

I thought he was joking. "Of course, I believe. Don't you?"

"No. Absolutely not." He wasn't smiling now. "You can't believe that. Just who do you think made God?"

My mouth fell open. I suddenly felt cold. I didn't try to answer him or argue. I just wanted to get away from him. "Take me back to the sorority house."

Although he called repeatedly, I no longer had any positive feeling toward him and refused to take his calls. It was as if someone had used a knife to cut us apart. I never dated him again.

Next I dated a football player who was in my English literature class. Both of us struggled to understand what the professor saw in the stories we read. So I was concerned about the first exam.

But in the football dorm my new boyfriend found a file of the teacher's previous exams. I memorized those answers and studied all my notes. The test was identical to the one in the files.

The professor passed out the graded exams, but he didn't record the grades until the papers were turned back in to him, so he thought none of his tests had ever left his classroom.

Before each quiz, the football player found an old test on the material covered. Soon, we just memorized the answers and stopped studying. We always made As. There was even a final exam on file.

But when the final exam was handed out, it was a completely different test. Not a single question was the same. What was I to do? All I could do was write the answers I had memorized for the other test. So I started writing and filled up two blue books, which were notebooks given out for test answers.

As I turned them in, the professor said, "Did you make your usual 'A', Miss Padgett?"

"I hope so."

The next morning the grades were posted. I made an 'A' on the final and an 'A' in the course. He never opened my first test booklet. The first line would have given me away. I don't know how the football player did on the final, but he failed my marriage test. He was just too dishonest.

It was years before I realized how I had been protected from marrying someone of another faith, someone of no faith, or someone who was so dishonest, even though I was all of those.

As my remaining days in college decreased, I feared time was running out. I hadn't found a husband. When I graduated, the mate pool would be a lot smaller. I began to pray earnestly that God would send Mr Right into my life. It didn't happen.

I just don't measure up. Only those lacking want me. I don't have the qualities to get the attributes I demand.

My last college boyfriend gave me his fraternity pin, usually a pre-engagement sign. He was from a wealthy, socially prominent, Mobile family. His parents came unannounced to my home in Birmingham to check out me and my parents. We apparently failed to measure up, because shortly after he asked for his pin back.

I know I'm looking too hard for love, but I'm scared. I worry that I'll always be alone. I must be expecting too much for what I have to offer. I'm afraid after I leave the Happy Hunting Grounds here at the University I'll never find anyone that even comes close to my ideal mate.

Daddy had been right after all. I did get the B.A. title but not the Mrs. So I accepted a job as a reporter for the Tampa (Florida) Times. Judy Hinton, my college roommate and Comella Hinton, Judy's cousin and my big sister in sorority, were moving to Florida with me. They would be teaching school. I was sure HE would be there too.

Anne Moss met her future husband when she was in high school. One night when she got home from the football game, her mother asked her, "Guess who came by tonight? George Moss. He wanted to take you to the football game. But when you weren't here he took me!" So Anne's mother actually went in her place on their planned first date.

Then when Anne married George, his parents lived in Miami. George thought Florida was a great place for a honeymoon and since his parents lived there he wouldn't have to pay for a place to stay.

"His parents gave us their bedroom in their two bedroom house," Anne remembered. "When we went in and closed the door I wondered what they were thinking. We had to be very quiet. They were sleeping nearby.

"In three months I was pregnant and I didn't even know how to boil water."

Baby number one, a girl named Deryl was born, followed by George Jr., fifteen months later.

"We found out what caused it so it was several years before we had Carl, Karen and Donna. Donna drown as a toddler in a neighbor's swimming pool. Then later Karen recovered from a serious head injury in a wreck where one of the drivers died after skidding on the ice. Life isn't always easy."

When Anne and George became Christians they joined the nearby Briarwood Presbyterian Church. For years they hosted the covered dish dinners for each session of Evangelism Explosion and served the church and community in others ways.

Chapter 5

I SAT THE last of my suitcases down and looked around at my new home. Some previous tenant preferred sitting on the right side of the brown, tweed sofa, where the cushions were permanently flattened. Burns, allowing the lining to show through, meant they had been smokers as did the odor. The end tables even matched with their own burns and circular water marks. Since I didn't have a television I put my clock radio on the TV table beside the green vinyl chair, which had one small tear. Only the overhead light illuminated the room; there was no lamp, picture or any other accessory. Dingy gray walls, well worn, stained carpet and venetian blinds completed the decor. That was all I could afford - $60 a month rent for this "furnished" apartment. It would take well over a fourth of my monthly salary. And this was the best I had seen for that amount. It would be a push with the monthly $75 car payment. And I would still have to pay for food, electricity, water, and gasoline for the car. I couldn't afford a telephone; I'd use the pay phone down on the first floor. No one who would be calling me anyway. Besides, I would have hated for someone to pick me up at this dump.

If I only had a roommate I could afforded something nicer. But I was totally alone. Neither Judy nor Comella had moved to Florida. Judy was marrying Glenn Bishop and Comella changed her mind. And the Y.W.C.A. had burned shortly before I arrived.

I could still smell the spaghetti sauce which greeted me in the central hall. It overpowered the other supper cooking odors, reminding me I had to buy breakfast food before I started my job tomorrow. I didn't want to be out after dark in this neighborhood where old cars were abandoned on properties, weeds took the place of grass and everything needed a coat of paint.

My strange, u-shaped apartment in the Wilton Arms had two entrances to the one bedroom, living room, kitchen and two bathrooms unit. I never felt quite safe and the fact that the police searched the building once and the fire marshal checked out the apartments for fire hazards, didn't help my apprehensions.

I usually took a sandwich for lunch and ate in the newspaper's cafe. When people didn't eat their unopened crackers, I took them. Before long there was a notice on the bulletin board, "Save your crackers for Jo Anne." I wasn't embarrassed; I was happy to get them. Increasingly, I was assigned lunch or dinner meetings. I really appreciated those assignments right before payday, when my money was gone. Then I lived on black pepper sandwiches - bread, mayonnaise and black pepper.

I'm going home. I can't stand it here. I never go anywhere except to work. I live in this hovel. I'll stay one more month. But if it doesn't get better, I'm leaving.

I was assigned to interview Fabian, a popular teen idol, singer and movie star, who was giving a performance in the nearby city of Clearwater. There was nothing in the newspaper's library about him so I would have to ask very basic questions. As I was thinking about what I would ask and looking for the auditorium in Clearwater, I was almost through the intersection before I noticed the red traffic light. It was mounted on the side of the street instead of in the middle. Then, I heard the siren and saw the police car in my rear view mirror.

"I'm sorry, officer, I'm not used to traffic lights on the side of the street." I tried to explain as I handed him my driver's license. Thankfully, it was a Florida license. The previous month when I wrote about the Highway Patrol, they insisted I pass the Florida driver's test right then.

"Where are you from?" the policeman asked. "I see you have an Alabama tag."

"I live in Tampa. The car is in my parents' name in Birmingham."

"Just follow me down to the police station."

There I was told that since I was from out of town, I would have to pay the $10 fine now. I looked in my purse but I only had fifty cents. I didn't have a checking account or a credit card.

"I'm sorry I don't have enough money. I'll have to pay the ticket when I get paid."

"No. The fine must be paid tonight. You'll have to call someone to bring you the money."

"There is no one I can call. I'm in a new job and I don't know anyone that well."

"Then, you'll have to go to jail."

To book me, they took my photograph and as they were taking my fingerprints I exploded. "So this is the way you treat strangers to your city. I'm not a derelict. I'm a newspaper reporter in Tampa, which is just 30 miles away. I'm going to write a story about your treatment of visitors to your city. They will run it in Tampa. My father works for a newspaper in Birmingham. They will run it too. Then, the Associated Press will pick it up and soon the whole nation will be warned about being a tourist in Clearwater."

"Have a seat over there. I'll go and talk to the sergeant."

In a few minutes the officer returned and told me their decision. "We are going to let you go on your own recognizance. But if you don't pay your fine before your court date, we'll come and arrest you."

I was late for my interview with Fabian. It didn't go well, but I managed to get enough information to write something. I considered writing about my experiences in Clearwater anyway, but decided it was best not to antagonize the police.

Winter comes to mid Florida too. When it got cold I never had an extra $25 for the deposit to have the gas turned on in my apartment. To get warm I'd get in bed under my electric blanket. I gladly accepted any baby sitting jobs I got from people at work, not only for the money but to be able to watch TV and to be warm. Gasoline was less than 50 cents a gallon. Many times after work, to keep from going to my cold, silent rooms, I would drive out to the causeway on the upper part of Tampa Bay to watch the sunset over the water.

Is this going to be my life? Always alone. Never having anyone care for me. If I couldn't find one person to love me when I was in school, where most are unmarried, how can I ever hope to find him out here in this big, big world. I'd rather be dead than for it to continue like this.

Of course, I never expressed these thoughts to my parents or let them know how I struggled financially. I was determined to make it on my own. But I sure was lonesome. I realized how little I had valued my family and friends. I missed having people who cared for me or even someone to talk to.

The women editor at the newspaper knew a girl who was looking for someone to share her apartment. After work I drove out to see the place and meet Sally Rucker. Located in a residential area of sweeping lawns with live oaks, decked with Spanish moss, various palms, and other tropical shrubs, this neighborhood looked like Heaven after my long months in the tenement.

"We'll share the living room and kitchen but you'll have your own bedroom and bath, the one down the hall on the left," Sally Rucker said after inviting me in. "I'll be living here only six months until my marriage. Then, you would have to find your own roommate. Look around and see what you think."

I could see how she found a husband with her clean cut, perky looks and welcoming smile. About my age and size, around 100 pounds, she wore her dark hair in a pony tail with bangs. She seemed like she would be easy to live with and the apartment was elegant. No bare walls, torn-up furniture or missing accessories here.

"This is so beautiful. Did you add all these decorations?"

"No, the owner did it all. Edwina Blake lives upstairs, right over us. She is the head interior decorator for Moss Brothers, that large department store downtown."

"I'd love to live here but I'm afraid I may not be able to afford it. What's the rent?"

"Your half would be $60 plus half the utilities."

For the same price I was paying I could live in a safe, warm, beautiful place with someone to talk to, a television to watch and even a telephone.

Everything got better after I moved to my new address on Villa Rica. At work I was given the federal government beat. And Sally's fiancee got me a blind date.

John Cheek, from Ft. Smith, Ak, had recently finished medical school and was stationed in Tampa at McDill Air Force Base. About 5'10" with a medium build, he had blond hair and eyes so blue I could swim in them. His face was that of a young boy up to some mischief. The few wrinkles on his forehead were not from playing golf in the sun, his main hobby, but from the peculiar way he had of raising his eyebrows when he wished to stress a point. I had never seen anything but old doctors; I didn't know they came in young, virile packages. I liked him even before he took me to Bern's for a Chateaubriand steak dinner by candlelight. It may have been the wine, the long time without social conversations or the confidence brought to me by my new surroundings, but my shyness disappeared and I was able to talk and talk and talk.

It was still early that warm, Spring night when we left the restaurant and he suggested we ride along the causeway between Tampa and Clearwater. On either side of the road the water lapped hungrily at the beach and the full moon sprinkled highlights on each ebb and flow and softly lit the scene.

"It's so beautiful. Can we park for a minute?" I asked him.

He pulled the car off the road. I sat looking over my right shoulder at the landscape of red hibiscus, amid patches of palmetto, beside the sand and water. I felt his arm pull me to him.

"No. No. This isn't what I meant," I said, shaking my head. "I mean I didn't intend for you to park in that sense of the word. It's just that it is so beautiful and the night is so tranquil ... I ... I didn't want the moment to pass."

He laughed. "You funny child. I know you didn't ..." but he never finished the sentence. That first kiss was so sweet, not hurrying, demanding or exploring as they would become.

Thus began our romance. He would be in Tampa for another year to finish his commitment to the government. Until 1973, when conscription was discontinued, men between the ages of 18 and 25 were drafted for two years military service. College and graduate students could get a deferment until graduation. When John's time in the service was over, he would be moving to Ann Arbor, Michigan for a residency in dermatology. I had a year to win him.

Please, Lord let this be the one.

Date followed date. The chit-chat became less important and shorter. If conversation and attraction sagged a little during the date it picked up in the final stretch until our emotions were demanding more than I could consciously give. It became harder and harder. The scales were now tipped toward the physical. But I remembered that Mama said a man never buys what he can get for free.

The showdown came one night watching TV at his apartment. The fact that I had too much to drink may have been the reason I chose to pour out my heart to him, but I didn't mean for it to overflow into tears.

"I'm so tired of trying to make ends meet on my salary. I wanted to prove that I could support myself but I'm giving up. I'm going home," I said aloud, but thought, *Please tell me to stay. Tell me you can bear for us to be apart.*

John switched to his doctor mode. "It would be a mistake to go home. You need to stick it out. If you go home you won't grow up; you'll remain a child. But it's your decision."

That's not what I want to hear.

When he saw that I was crying he tried to comfort me. That led to kisses and soon the hot embraces. But my mind still refused and I told him, "No. No. Stop."

He was so angry. "I'm taking you home." Nothing more was said until he walked me to the door. "If you ever need me, call."

I felt he would never ask me out again. But I hoped and waited and waited ... But he didn't call.

"John, I need you. You told me to call if I needed you and I do. Please come."

That was all he wanted to hear. "I'll be there shortly. See you real soon."

"I'm so ..." I didn't get to finish my sentence. He had hung up. It was Saturday afternoon, three weeks after our last date and I had not talked to him since. My roommate was out of town for the weekend so I was alone on the couch when he arrived.

"Come in. The door's open."

But when he took one look at me, he asked, "What's wrong? Are you sick?"

"My stomach is cramping. I can't stop vomiting. I've got a little diarrhea. I tried to tell you on the phone but you had hung up."

"How long has this been going on?" he asked as he felt my forehead and the pulse in my wrist.

"I started vomiting in the middle of the night and I've been sick ever since."

"Let me examine your abdomen. What have you eaten?"

"Just a little leftover tuna casserole last night that I had made earlier in the week."

Since I had minimal tenderness, not just located in the right lower quadrant of my abdomen, where the appendix is, he felt sure it was food poisoning. He went out and got Pepto Bismol which began calming my stomach almost immediately. He stayed with me all afternoon while I mostly slept.

"I feel so much better. Thank you for coming. I don't know what I would have done without you."

"I'm almost glad you got sick," he said as he put his arm around me. "I've been a stubborn fool. I love you. I wanted to call but I wouldn't. I don't want to argue any more; I won't put any more pressure on you."

The time flew and it seemed that suddenly John was leaving for

Ann Arbor. I silently steeled myself for his departure. I couldn't let him know how his leaving was destroying me.

"Jo Anne, I'm going to miss you. You are a wonderful girl."

Then, why don't you take me with you. You know I care for you and you've told me that you love me but you haven't made the commitment. Why? What's wrong with me? You are like the others. They like me, even say they love me, but not enough to want me for a wife. Those thoughts quickly went through my head but I only said, being noncommittal, "I'll miss you too. Maybe you'll drop me a line sometime."

"Of course. We'll stay in touch."

Chapter 6

IT WAS FIVE weeks of agony with only a couple of informational type letters when he called. "Could you fly up for a Michigan football weekend? You'll stay with a married couple. He's in residency with me."

The weekend was a blur of red, orange, green and gold as the leaves dressed for the coming change and the nip in the air teased that something was about to happen. The only discordant sound came from the losing football fans. For once we didn't argue about my smoking. Since he didn't smoke he was always on my case, urging me to stop. I purposely didn't smoke on this trip. Our time together was perfect. He must have thought so, because he asked me if I would spend Christmas in Arkansas with his family.

He wants me to meet his family. Unbelievable.

I liked his school teacher mother and contractor father and they seemed to really like me. Maybe they knew their only child's intentions because on Christmas Eve he asked me to marry him.

"I thought you told me you were never going to get married until you hit 72." I reminded him. "I figured that was way to late for marriage."

"You silly goose. I was talking about golf. I meant I wasn't going to marry until I hit par on the golf course."

I realized I wasn't dreaming. It had finally happened. God had finally answered my prayers.

God answered a friend's prayer about Bonnie Furuto. Bonnie, going to perform in Gadsden, AL., was riding with another violinist, who was in the Alabama Symphony with her. He was appalled that she was still playing a student violin. But with three sons in college it wasn't possible for her to buy a new one at that time. That friend was praying that God would provide a professional quality violin for her.

In Gadsden she learned a lady wanted to sell her recently deceased aunt's lovely violin and an amazing bow. Bonnie knew she couldn't afford the violin but asked the price of the bow.

"My aunt said they were not to be sold separately," the seller said. "And she specified they were to be used for the glory of God and the happiness of others. I'm convinced you are the one who is to have this violin," she told Bonnie. "I'm going to sell the violin and the bow for the cost of the bow and you can take as long as you need to pay me."

What a gift from God. Psalms 37:4 in the NIV Study Bible says "Delight yourself in the Lord and he will give you the desires of your heart." (All Bible quotations are from this Bible.)

I'm going to be a bride and like the story books say, live happily ever after. I didn't answer immediately. I had to take it all in. Savor the moment. Pinch myself. He was smiling with those perfect teeth. He knew my answer.

We'd marry the next fall, plenty of time for planning the wedding. I would give the newspaper a month's notice, then move to Michigan to be near him.

The two feet of snow made Ann Arbor look like a beautiful Currier and Ives card but the 10 degree temperature sucked your breath away, bringing you back to reality. I enrolled at Eastern Michigan University to get a teaching certificate and got a job as society editor for the Ypsilanti Daily Press, in the town adjoining Ann Arbor. I found a place to board in a home near the school, my job and the man I loved. We mainly saw each other on the weekends due to our studies.

The newspaper allowed me to work around my class time and the work wasn't hard. Another woman wrote all the material for the Wednesday food page. I wrote the engagements, weddings and an occasional feature story. But I mainly filled the women's pages with prewritten stories and shorts from a news service.

At Eastern Michigan I took two easy education classes and philosophy. In the latter class we discussed if flowers felt pain when you cut their stems, if they suffered separation anxiety when they were taken from the other flowers and similar topics. We never had an exam and our whole grade would be based on one paper. We could write about anything, in any form and of any length. Was it to be a research paper with footnotes? It was up to us. The professor wouldn't be specific.

In the education classes the teaching of a subject by rote memorization of the material was frowned upon. But that had been my whole education. I literally memorized my way through school. I felt I couldn't teach what I had never done - teaching concepts and letting the students draw their own conclusions. So for my philosophy paper I wrote about why I was not going to be a teacher, since I could only teach like I had been taught. It may have been my frankness that got me the 'A' but I always felt he gave everyone an 'A' so he wouldn't have to read any of the papers.

Although at the time I questioned the nonsense presented in the philosophy class, I accepted the education class ideas that boiled down to letting the students determine truth.

"What is truth?" Pilate asked Christ in John 18:38 NIV. This has been the foremost question throughout the ages. Jesus said, "I am the

Truth" (John 14:6 NIV) and that everyone on the side of truth listens to him. Later I heard Pastor Tom Cheely, say, "The Bible doesn't contain the truth, it is the truth."

Moving from Florida I suffered in the freezing temperatures. March did not bring any let up of the snows and spring did not arrive in April. It would be two more months until it suddenly was hot.

I flew home one weekend and Mother and one of her sisters decided to drive me back since the roads were no longer icy. I noticed a Blue Cross/Blue Shield insurance card with my name on it laying on the TV. Since I was a student my parents could carry me on their hospital insurance.

"Is this for me?" I asked Mother.

"Yes, take it. I had planned to mail it."

Arriving back in Michigan on Sunday, I felt miserable. I got sicker as the pain localized in my stomach. John diagnosed it as appendicitis and arranged for surgery. When you are young you never think of being admitted to a hospital. It was so fortunate that I went home that weekend and got my insurance card. I needed it before it could have reached me through the mail. And it wasn't a coincidence that Mother was there for the operation. God was in control.

After the surgery I couldn't straighten up due to the pain. It was a long time before I could stand up straight. It was not an easy recovery. But God looked after me, although at the time I didn't recognize his care and control of my circumstances.

As the semester ended, my parents were going to New York City for the World's Fair and asked if I wanted to fly over and join them. John said "go"; he needed to study for exams. Mother loved giveaways and had gotten tickets for us to attend "The Price Is Right" television program, the day before going to the fair. After the telecast anyone that wanted to be a contestant remained in the studio. They called on random people to tell their names, where they were from and how much they would bid for a piece of costume jewelry. From those people about ten were selected to be interviewed for selection for the next day's show. Four people competed for all the prizes: the returning champion who had won the most on the previous day, two new contestants and a guest celebrity, who played for names drawn from the audience. I was interviewed but I was not chosen for the following day's show. I was too much like the returning champion, a young, single, blond female.

Early the next day my family went to the World's Fair. I had a headache and told them if I felt better I would meet them at the main entrance at noon. I recovered by midmorning and called ABC and learned that if they had unfilled seats, they took people off the street to complete the audience. I got in, was interviewed and chosen to be on the next program on Monday.

I lived in furnished apartments and had never really bought much of anything. From watching the programs Mother knew a lot of the things they gave away, so that weekend we went to department stores and I made lists of the prices of possible prizes. For instance, a living room suite cost about $350 and a car around $3000. I crammed as if I was taking an exam, memorizing the prices of the possible items, that I might be bidding on.

Monday I was seated next to the guest celebrity, Milt Kamen, Sid Caesar's look-alike. He had sweat on his forehead so I offered him a Kleenex. I hadn't won anything when the last item, a travel trailer came up. At that time the rules prevented contestants from bidding between the bids of others. You had to be at least $100 or more over the previous bid. I bid $2,000 and Mr. Kamen bid $3,000 for the travel trailer. His bid gave me a $1,000 range and I won. I wondered if my offering him the tissue caused him to give me a greater chance to win. Winning the trailer made me the big winner.

On Tuesday's program I won everything given away: a moose head, a $1,000+ Oleg Cassini, full length, zebra coat, a trip to the Bahamas for two, a living room suite consisting of a couch, tables and two chairs, a sewing basket full of sewing notions and a boat, motor and trailer. The next day I won was a new car, a Pontiac Catalina.

The next day I didn't win anything. My total winnings were over $12,000, quite a haul in those days. But, things don't make you happy.

It was like a dream. I returned to Michigan with only the zebra coat; everything else was shipped to Birmingham. I had made the front page of the Ypsilanti Daily Press and also the Birmingham News the days I was on the show.

Of course, I had called John and told him all about it. On TV he watched me accumulate the prizes. But when I got back, he seemed distant and not very excited about my winnings. A few days later it all came out.

"Jo Anne, I hate to tell you, but I must. I'm having second thought about our marriage."

"What? Is there someone else?"

"No, there's no one," he said as he rubbed his chin. "It's hard to say. I can't put it in words but I feel we are not right for each other. It would be better to break up now than after we were married."

Being struck by a truck would have hurt less. I stood there looking at him and thinking, *I don't know this man. What happened to the one who loved me? How can he change so quickly?*

"How can you say that, John? Are you sure? I thought you loved me." The tears that filled my eyes now began their decent down my cheeks.

"I do love you. You are a wonderful girl." He began to wipe away my tears. "But it's better this way."

"You can't love me and not want to spend the rest of your life with me. I love you and that's what I want."

"Jo Anne, I don't want to hurt you. But I think it is over."

"Please, don't do this to me. You can't be sure. You could change your mind again."

"No, I don't think so. It's probably best if you move back to Alabama."

I wanted to scream, stomp my foot and tell him he had to love me. *How can I live without him? How can he say or do this to me. I hate the dirty rat.*

"You had me leave a good job and move up here. You are worse than contemptible. I hope you get paid back." My anger poured out as I tried to hurt him like he had hurt me. "I hope you have a miserable life."

Lord, you know I don't mean it. Please change him mind. I can't live without him.

But the engagement was broken. Nothing would change that. Devastated and dejected, I returned to Birmingham to walk the floor crying as I tried to analyze what went wrong.

"John, I love you. I love you with all my heart. Please, come back to me. I won't suffocate you by demanding so much attention. It was just that I've been so lonely these past two years, so far from relatives and friends. I realize how terribly spoiled I was - not with possessions but with relationships. I learned in Florida I needed more than a dream job and a nice apartment. I was so thankful for your love but I needed, wanted and even demanded more of your time. I promise I'll no longer be jealous of your two other loves - medicine and golf." I put down my pen. I knew I couldn't mail this letter. I felt so much had to be said, but I wasn't the one to initiate it. I would wait.

I'll never find anyone, I thought as I cried. *I must be terrible. I've prayed for a husband for years, starting in college. Why, God, why can't I find someone to love me? This is like death. I'll never see him again. I was so happy and now it's over. What will I do with the rest of my life? There'll never be anyone else. No one could measure up to his attributes. No, the problem is I don't measure up.*

I had been home two months. I was miserable. Was he? Was he still sure this was the right thing to do? He might have changed his mind. I swallowed my pride and telephoned him. He hadn't. In fact, he was engaged to a nurse.

"Isn't that strange. I've met someone too, also a doctor. And like you he loves golf," I said through my tears. "But, unlike you, he has beautiful brown eyes and thick, black hair."

I didn't want him to know how devastated I was, so I lied. I thought there wasn't much chance of my finding someone like that. Little did I know I had just described my future husband.

Mother was glad we had broken up. She had never liked John's blond hair. All of our children would have been blonds and she didn't want that.

I should have known; she doesn't like blonds, even if her daughter is one.

"You'll find someone else," she assured me. But I doubted it.

Single men were concentrated in universities, so I decided to go back to graduate school. With my winnings I couldn't afford to work any more that year or I would go into a higher tax bracket. If I was a full-time student Daddy could count me as a dependent on his income tax. So the "Price Is Right" was the impetus behind my return to school. I got the M.A. degree but again, not the real title I was seeking.

Although in years I was 23 when I moved to Michigan, I was only a teenager. Now I felt like an old woman at 24. It's hard to believe so many important dreams were realized and shattered in such a short time. Life goes on, they say, but I'll just be going through the motions. I'll find a job, but if that's all I have to look forward to, then I don't want any future.

Chapter 7

"MOTHER, I HAD the most wonderful dream."

"Not another one about John."

"No, I dreamed I was on "the Price Is Right" again."

"Well, that one is just as impossible as any you've had about him."

I was looking for a job when ABC called, inviting me to be a contestant on their first "Price Is Right Return of Champions" show. They would pay for travel and accommodations. Mother and I returned to New York where I won a trip to London for two. They gave all the contestants a silver tray, engraved with the event name and date, 1964.

The main expense in visiting Europe in the 60s was the round-trip ticket. Both my parents could go since they only had to buy one fare. We bought a Volkswagen in Birmingham to be picked up at the German factory. That saved enough money to pay for our travel around Europe and even to ship the car home.

Our 'wonderland' trip began with the free week in London and side trips to see Canterbury Cathedral near the white cliffs of Dover and Shakespeare's home in Stratford-in-Avon. Then we picked up the car in Frankfort and drove through seven European countries. We wanted to go to Italy but Mother had read that real bargains were to be found in Andorra, a tiny country sandwiched between France and Spain in the Pyrenees Mountains. Since this was her only request, we drove through the south of France, up the two lane road through the mountains to Andorra. There are no bargains there - in fact there's nothing there, except one small town, the capital, also named Andorra.

But we saw memorial sights in southern France. Built in the fifth century, Carcassonne is a perfect example of a medieval, walled town. It is surrounded by a moat with a draw bridge for entry onto its cobblestone streets.

In the Rhone valley we saw the perfectly preserved arena, temple and other Roman ruins in Nimes. At Pont du Gard we studied the aqueduct and Roman bridge.

We also relived the horrors of World War II as we walked through burned ruins of the French village of Oradour-sur-Glane. Not a single inhabitant escaped. Most were burned alive in a church because the Germans thought the residents had helped American soldiers escape capture. The tiny village was left as it was on June 10, 1944.

In southern France we stopped where a man was harvesting grapes. Using a phrase book, we tried to buy some. He gave us a huge amount but wouldn't take any money. We ate the grapes and threw the seeds in the floor of the Volkswagen. When it arrived back in the states, Mother found the seeds, planted them and grew grapes from France. That was the real bargain she got from going to Andorra.

We stayed in people's homes whenever we could. It was cheaper and you could really see how they lived. The beds were equipped with eiderdown comforters. They were even better than an electric blanket. One cost around $100, more than I could afford. It was years before they were available here.

Our favorite place was Berchesgaden in the German Bavarian Alps, near the boarder with Austria. This picturesque, sparkling clean town with friendly people is the locale of Hitler's Eagle's Nest, which we visited along with the salt mines.

Back home, I found a job doing statistical research, even though the last math class I had was high school geometry. My boss, paid by a government grant, didn't seem to care that I couldn't do math. After a couple of months he went on a trip leaving me in charge of the office. I continued writing up the results of his research until the day I opened his top desk drawer and found nude pictures of him and other staff members. Now, I understood why he didn't care about my math ability. I did no more work. I cleared out my desk, and the day he returned, I demanded and got a letter of recommendation before I left. I had threatened to call his wife.

I was still praying and pleading with God for a husband. I decided to give one more shot at finding a mate at a place where men were concentrated. But I was running out of schools. I applied, took the test and was accepted at Cumberland School of Law at Samford University in Birmingham.

I took night classes because I had a new job as the customer representative for Xerox Corporation with a great salary and an expense account. I taught customers how to use their new copier. Later I visited them to see if there were any problems. I kept a notebook on the people who were in charge of the Xerox machine in each location, their families, pets, hobbies and other facts. I would refresh my memory from my cheat sheets before I entered their office. Everyone likes to be remembered.

The second week one of the salesmen, took me along to visit some of his accounts. The Veteran's Hospital used Xerox paper in their EKG machine. I had never seen an EKG test so I stood in the hall and watched through the open door as the electrodes were taped to the patient's chest. The salesman walked away to try to sell more paper to his contact.

Down the hall came the most handsome man I had ever seen. He was wearing the long white coat of a physician. With mahogany brown eyes and hair as black as coal he looked like a Greek god. I thought, *he's probably Jewish. And he is too good looking to be single*. He entered the room with the EKG machine.

When he came out of the patient's room, he walked over to me and said, "Hi. My name is Roy Roddam. I'm a doctor and I'm single. I was wondering if you would like to have dinner with me."

"I would."

My quick answer surprised me as much as his brash proposition. Even though I didn't know him, I knew I could find out about him. I had two unmarried sorority sisters who worked at the medical center and they would know all the good looking, single doctors. *They'll know if he's really single ... they'll know about this one.*

"Wonderful," he said. How about this Saturday night?"

"I'm free Saturday."

He pulled out a little notebook and added, "Oh, what's your name? I'll need your address and phone number too."

I gladly told him.

My friends, Patsy Schell, a dietitian, and Martha Mullins, a medical technologist, certainly did know who he was and yes, they would go out with him, if he asked. But they warned me he was a real playboy.

That Saturday in January we woke up to a record nine inch snow accumulation. The toilet paper salesman, I was dating, called to see if I wanted to play in the snow. With a job like that, he had a great sense of humor and was fun to be with, but I kept refusing his marriage proposals. We went to a hilly golf course and spent the afternoon riding metal trays down the inclines, making a snowman and pelting each other with snowballs.

I barely got home in time to get ready for my date with the doctor. We were to go out to dinner and then to an operatic performance of Cinderella. I quickly bathed but my hair looked awful. All that playing in the snow made my fine textured hair as limp as cooked spaghetti.

I heard the door bell ring and Mother inviting him into the den. As Mother and Daddy were talking with him, I tried to do something with my hair.

"Your date is here, Jo Anne." Mother came to tell me.

"I know. I heard you let him in but I've had to roll my hair to give it a little curl." "I thought you played too long in the snow."

"I know I did, now."

"It's getting too late for you to go out to eat and still make the play. Want me to offer him some chili that I cooked for supper?"

"Yes, please, and bring me a bowl, too. I'll take my hair down in a few minutes."

When I took the pins out, my hair looked like I had played in the snow all day - just horrid. I was so mad at myself. Here was my big chance to go out with this wonderful man and I'd blown it. I knew better but I just went ahead and kept having fun. *Why was I always like that - living in the moment? I never could give up present pleasures for future gains. Who would want to be seen with someone that looked like I did?*

"Jo Anne, what are you doing?" Mother was back at the bathroom door. "That poor man has been waiting close to an hour."

"I'll just not go. Tell him to go on ..."

"You get out of there. He's been very patient. You need to leave now to get to the play on time."

Well, when he sees my hair, that will be the last time I see him. I went to my messy room with the clothes, I had worn earlier, on the floor and several dresses I had decided not to wear, thrown on the bed. I closed the door to my room. *At least, I'll have something to talk about. This Oleg Cassini coat, won on the television show, is sure to impress him.* But I was soon to learn he had an even better claim to fame.

Roy, born April 9, 1935 was the only child born to Mildred and Marvin Roddam. After he was born his parents may have felt one child was enough, or it may have been because he was so perfect, as only children always are. Raised in the Woodlawn area of Birmingham, Roy told me about his years spent at the University of Alabama preparing for medical school. He received his M.D. degree in 1959, one year after I graduated from high school.

After his internship and a couple of years of residency in Internal Medicine, he had to serve in the military. He went into the Air Force as a captain.

"I was a flight surgeon, stationed at Hickam Air Force Base in Hawaii on November 22, 1963, when President John Kennedy was assassinated," Roy told me. "Kennedy's cabinet, their wives and aides were flying to Japan for a meeting on Asian economics with their Japanese counterparts. After receiving the news about the president from the onboard teletype machine, the jet turned around and returned to Hickam. They asked for a doctor to fly back to Washington D.C. with them. I was that physician."

"Tell me about it."

"It was mainly uneventful, a precautionary measure since so many of them were close to President Kennedy. They couldn't believe the tragedy. Like most onboard, I mainly watched the ticker tape telling about the developments in Dallas and someone named Lee Harvey Oswall. Secretary of State Dean Rusk apologized for jerking me out of my duty station. On arrival in D.C. I watched through the window as Dean Rusk gave an impromptu press conference. Then, I caught another military transport back to Hawaii."

It was a wonderful date. Apparently he didn't notice my hair. When I got home Mother asked me what I thought of him.

"That's who I'm going to marry."

"Don't get your hopes up."

Roy asked me out for the next weekend but I was already committed to attending a sorority sister's wedding in south Alabama. I asked if he wanted to drive me there and back. He agreed.

Now, my problem was what I would talk to him about on that long trip. I was never very good at small talk. But we had stacks of Reader's Digest in the basement. I went through Reader's Digest magazines and wrote the best jokes on index cards, and then memorized them. Whenever there was a lull in the conversation, I told him a joke.

"You are the funniest person I have ever known."

Every time we went out, I had to memorize new jokes.

I had always heard that God gives us what we are asking for or something better. I prayed that he'd be the answer to my prayers.

On the long drive to and from the wedding, I learned a lot about him.

"There are two things I can't stand," he told me, "a smoker and someone who doesn't pick up after themselves."

He didn't know I smoked. The other doctor didn't like my smoking. So I waited to see if this one smoked, before I lit up. Smoking was everywhere in 1966 so everyone smelled like cigarettes. Roy never asked me if I smoked; he just assumed I didn't. Thankfully, I played it smart about the cigarettes.

I could probably win the Messiest Person Award. I made a mental note to make sure my bedroom door was always closed.

I knew he was what I wanted - someone with more degrees than I had, good looking and successful. But he didn't know what he'd be getting - both the things he hated most. Life is like that. Sometimes you get the very things you don't want. It would help him grow.

Roy was in the last year of his residency in Internal Medicine. He worked all night, every other night, during the week at the University Hospital after his regular daytime duties. The nights he was off, he moon-lighted at East End Hospital for extra cash. On the weekends he dated me. The playboy reputation was just one of the many un-true rumors that circulated through the hospital like blood pulsating through the body.

In a couple of months he asked me to marry him. My happiness knew no bounds. My mood soared into the atmosphere as I began to plan a June wedding. But one night he confessed that he felt we were moving too fast; he was having second thoughts, as he remembered his five year marriage with an unfaithful wife.

They had no children and tests revealed it was due to his low sperm count. So he had warned me that we could never have children of our own; we would have to adopt.

"I can't make another mistake. Maybe we better put this off."

My world crashed. *This can't be happening again. I can't go through this I'll go crazy.* I tried to smile and be light about it but he could see my pain.

Seeing how much it hurt me, he soon began to relent and before long we were again planning our wedding. When we told his parents that we planned to marry, his mother said, "Well, it's your life."

Another person who thought I wasn't good enough. We began planning for it to happen anyway on June 3, 1966, a little more than five months after we met.

Our on again, off again wedding plans were sure different from Louie and Rebecca Haynes who went on their first date and decided to get married ... that night.

Louie Haynes was a 13 year old basketball player in junior high school, when he first saw Rebecca. She was a 13 year old cheerleader.

He didn't see her again until he was a senior in high school. Louie had been dating Rebecca's best friend, Beverly. But he wanted to date Rebecca. So Louie wrote two notes: one to Beverly telling her that he was breaking up with her and another to Rebecca, saying he wanted to date her. He had his young nephew deliver them. Neither note had a girl's name on it so the notes got mixed up. Beverly, the girl Louie was dating, got a note saying he wanted to date her. And Rebecca's note said he was breaking up with her.

"How strange," Rebecca thought, "I'm not even dating you.

Later her sister made a date for Rebecca with Louie. When he arrived for their date, she liked his looks and thought, "I'm going to marry that guy." A lot alike, they enjoyed the same things, were both Baptist believers, and wanted the wife to stay home and take care of the two or so children, each planned on having.

"I guess I better take you home," Louie said.

"I really don't want to go home," Rebecca said. "What are we going to do?"

"The only thing I know is to get married," he answered.

"How are we going to do that? We are only 17. We'd have to have our parents' permission and there is a three day waiting period."

Those problems were solved by driving to Trenton, Ga., just south of Chattanooga. On the way, Rebecca asked him, "Do you love me?"

"I reckon I do. I'm marrying you."

They didn't have a honeymoon until two months later when two of their friends got married and asked if they wanted to go on their honeymoon with them. All four drove to Chattanooga and had adjoining motel rooms, separated by a shared bathroom.

If they weren't before, they now became very close friends.

That's how Rebecca and Louie got married on their first date and then later honeymooned with another couple. God was certainly active in that marriage that began 53 years ago.

Chapter 8

"HAPPY IS THE bride the sun shines on" the old adage goes. I was ecstatic that sunny day. First thing on my list was a trip to the beauty shop to get my first ever manicure and to have my long hair washed and pinned up into a French twist with deep waves on each side of my face.

Then Mother's oldest sister, Myrt, and I made net bags, filling them with rice for the guests to throw on us, as we left the reception. Showering the bride and groom with rice was supposed to bring fertility and prosperity.

In the mail was a letter from my favorite journalism professor. "When we got the invitation we first thought it was the Michigan doctor you were marrying, but we were informed it was another physician. I see you're determined to get free medical service for life."

He didn't know I would have settled for free legal advice. I had passed my finals for my night classes at Cumberland Law School the previous week. Not that it mattered. Now, I could drop out. I didn't need to attend any more schools. Daddy was happy - I kept getting more education. Of course, he was getting poorer by degrees.

Roy worked his regular day at the hospital before our 8 p.m. vows.

Judy Hinton Bishop, my best friend from college, who got married instead of moving to Florida with me, was my matron of honor. Judy was so beautiful with dark eyes and hair. She was confident in herself and thus lived on an even keel in contrast to my roller coaster emotions. She had a calming effect on me.

My other two attendants were Helen Cotter, my friend since grammar school, and Jane Blankenship Padgett, my sister-in law. We dressed at Trinity Methodist Church in Homewood, so our gowns wouldn't be wrinkled. I didn't have a flower girl. They are said to distract from the bride.

"Do you have something old, something new, something borrowed and something blue?" Judy joked as we got dressed.

"After waiting this long, do you think I would do anything to jeopardize my marriage. I'm wearing those old, comfortable, white satin heels, that we both wore to formals at Alabama. I even put a penny in one shoe for luck."

I looked at myself in the floor length mirror wearing my white organza wedding dress, trimmed with lace and pearls and made with an empire waist, cap sleeves and a short train.

"My wedding gown is the new item which shows hope for my new life."

The ninety-eight pounds on my five foot two inch frame didn't give a whole lot of curves. *At least*, I thought, *he can't see my legs. My brother said they were so skinny they looked like straws with olives for knees. My hair is the way Roy likes it, up on top of my head. It's styled just right to wear the Juliet cap of lace and pearls with a veil attached to it.*

"Jo Anne is wearing my pearl and diamond earrings," Helen said. "When the bride wears an item from a happily married friend, it transfers some of her good fortune to the bride. I've got plenty to share."

"Jane gave me a blue garter, the color of faithfulness, to wear," I said.

It was time to begin. The ushers, my brother and Roy's cousin, Dr. Tom Smitherman, walked down the aisle, followed by my attendants. Roy and the best man, his father, were waiting at the altar with the pastor of Trinity Methodist Church.

As the Bridal Chorus rang out, I entered the church on my right foot so our marriage would be off on the right start. For the first time that day I saw Roy. It's bad luck to see each other on your wedding day before the ceremony. I was raised with my mother's superstitions so I was familiar with everything you needed to do for good luck including never opening an umbrella in the house, putting a hat on the bed or walking under a ladder. I didn't know until years later that God controls all circumstances so there is no such thing as luck.

Roy was smiling but he was nervous as evidenced by the beads of sweat above his upper lip. The church was filled, but our vows seemed personal, as if we were standing there alone. I had to hold up Roy several times. I wondered if he was so scared that his knees were weak? No, he told me, he was confused as to when we were to kneel. When he did kneel you could read "help" on the bottom of one of his shoes. Quickly, it was over. The ultimate goal of my whole life had been met. I was finally married. We hurried out to begin our new life together, but only after the church reception.

Mother's sister, Myrt, had made the beautiful wedding cake and mints. That, with peanuts and punch, was all that was served at the church reception.

As we cut our wedding cake, I remembered the recent wedding of a sorority sister from New Jersey. She had married in her husband's small Alabama hometown. She brought her wedding cake and stored it in the motel room where she was staying. After the rehearsal the bride and the bridesmaids found the cake covered in ants. They put the cake on a luggage rack with each leg in a cup of water. Then, they drank beer while picking the ants off the cake so it could be served the next day.

After we posed for pictures and greeted the guests at our reception, I changed into my going away outfit - a pink, silk suit with a pink, Jackie Kennedy style pillbox hat, trimmed with net and tiny bows. A black patent purse and heels and white kid gloves completed my outfit. We ran through the shower of rice to Roy's car which was decorated with tin cans and old shoes tied to the back bumper. The windshield said "Slave" on the driver's side and "Slave Driver" over the passenger's side. Underneath it said, "Shut up and drive, stupid." We sped away, out-maneuvering and out running those blowing their horns as they followed us.

We drove into the garage of Roy's little house on College Avenue in the Homewood section of Birmingham and quickly shut the garage door. We didn't turn on the lights so no one would know we were there. We had to hold hands and feel our way in. And then we lit one small candle and drank champagne while sitting in bed. If you could bottle happiness there would have been a lot of bottles thrown under the bed that night.

Roy only had a couple of days off, so the next morning we headed to Calloway Gardens in Pine Mountain, Ga. for our honeymoon. It is a 2,500 acre garden with paved road threading past spring fed lakes and thousands of flowering plants. It also has three golf courses. Roy chose it because he had always wanted to play golf there. I didn't play golf. Maybe we saw the gardens. I don't remember. I just remember waiting in our Holiday Inn room four hours for him to return from playing 18 holes of golf. I did sneak out to smoke. Before his return I changed clothes, brushed my teeth, rinsed with Listerine and put on perfume. He loves golf so it was a toss up about what he enjoyed most on our honeymoon. For me it wasn't a hard choice.

I had it all. He was worth waiting for. I was so happy I was almost giddy. I couldn't do enough to please him. Mama had warned me not to start off doing anything I didn't want to do for the rest of our married life. But I paid no attention. He was so good I felt I could eat him. Later on, I wished I had. God certainly had answered my prayers ... even if it did take years. I don't remember if I thanked Him.

I continued working at Xerox. One afternoon I finished visiting clients early and went home, even though it wasn't quitting time. I was sitting on the back steps smoking when I looked around and saw Roy looking out the window at me.

"I can't believe it," he said through clinched teeth. "I wouldn't have married you if I had known you smoked."

Could he care that little about me? Would I lose him? I thought he wouldn't say that if he truly loved me.

I stiffened my back and didn't try to quit. But I never smoked in the house or in front of him. And I made sure I didn't smell like I had been smoking. Cigarettes were the first crack in our happiness.

Going home, after having dinner with some of his friends and their wives, I said, Did you notice what Joyce was wearing?

"No, what about it?"

"Well, it was so sexy. I would never wear something like that. It was so low cut and so tight she looked like she was advertising to be a call girl."

"I didn't think that."

"No wonder, she was flirting with you all night."

"What are you talking about? You shouldn't say things like that."

"Why not?"

"You just shouldn't."

"Then, I won't have anything to say."

"I mean don't say bad things about others. A good adage is, if you can't say something good, don't say anything."

"If I can't tell you, who can I tell?"

"Don't tell anybody."

I didn't argue anymore but I didn't like it. I though he was my best friend and now I would have to be careful what I said to him.

Not being a Christian, I didn't know that Romans 1:29-30 warns about the tongue's unrighteous behavior in committing malice and slander, among other things.

"Jo Anne, you've been crying. What's wrong?"

"I'm not pregnant. I started my period today."

"Oh, for goodness sakes," he said taking me in his arms, "we've only been married a month." Then, I heard the sadness in his voice, "Don't you remember I told you we will never have children of our own. We'll have to adopt."

"You can't be certain that we'll have to adopt."

Sue Price suspected she was adopted but didn't learn that it was true until late in life. She asked her aunt if that was true and was told, "I thought you knew that a long time ago." She wondered about her birth family and hoped to meet them someday.

She never asked her family about her adoption, but when the man she called "father" died, she looked for, but couldn't find, her adoption papers in his things. This was strange when he was known for keeping everything.

His wife, Sue's step mother, had Alzheimer's Disease. Sue planned to move her to another assisted living place so she contacted the woman's son. The son was concerned that he might end up like his mother with that dreaded disease.

He said to Sue, "Since you are adopted you don't have that to worry about."

"How do you know that?" she asked.

"Because I've got your adoption records."

When he sent Sue her records she found out her birth mother's name. Sue contacted her birth mother, who told Sue didn't want to have anything to do with her.

Sue did learn from her that she had an older brother. But her mother concealed the fact that Sue also had a older sister.

Sue's real brother and sister found Sue's letter to their mother after their birth mother died. They got Sue's children's names from that letter so they were able to contact her through Sue's oldest son, Frank.

In May, 2018 in Destin, FL, Sue, at age 70, met the sister she never knew existed. Their brother's medical problems prevented him from attending, but they have talked on several occasions. Only God could have brought them all together.

Roy just shook his head, not believing we would have our own child. But I was determined to pray for a child, just like I had asked God for a husband. The next month I was late. I didn't say a word. But two weeks later I couldn't contain myself. "I'm late. I must be pregnant."

"I don't think so. You'll start your period soon."

"You are wrong. I've never been late and I've never missed a period."

He didn't believe it even when the pregnancy test came back positive. But I was sure. Roy thought it was impossible until he got his stethoscope, placed it on my stomach and listened.

"I think I hear something," he said in amazement. "It can't be ... but I do hear another heartbeat besides yours. You really are pregnant."

And no wonder. It was good to be in your middle twenties, married to a man in his early thirties, both interested in grabbing all the gusto they could. That feeling didn't always wait for the privacy of the bedroom but would catch us uncontrollably on the highway, looking for that deserted, backwood's road or in Florida when that deserted lane turned out to be sand. We didn't care that we were completely stuck. We would worry about that later. Luckily, we noticed the flashing lights behind the car before the police officer walked to our car. I hid my face but I wanted to shout, "we're married," when the smiling cop leaned down to look in the window and offer assistance in getting us out of this jam. Oh, the perils of the newly weds.

When you are waiting for your first baby the time is long. Your first feelings are slight butterfly flutterings which grow stronger, evidencing the life growing inside of you. Yes, you are going to be a mother. It's an awesome feeling. You wonder if you can meet the coming responsibility of raising a good person.

You wonder what the baby will be, what it will look like and if it will be all right. Finally, you surrender and leave it in God's hands, where it was all the time.

The last three months are the longest. Now, you know you are expecting. The butterfly within has turned into a fish which flops and then into a kangaroo, trying out his kicks. Weekly doctor visits, intense hunger, watching your diet and your swelling feet won't let you forget. You look in the mirror and wonder if you will ever see that carefree, slim girl again. You probably won't.

I was glad to get into maternity clothes but as soon as I did, Xerox would no longer allow me to represent them "in my condition" so I began working in the office.

Chapter 9

OUR LITTLE HOMEWOOD bungalow had two bedrooms, one of which Roy used as an office. So with no room for the baby we looked for a larger house which we found when I was eight and a half months pregnant. We moved almost immediately. I had a week to get unpacked.

I woke up around 3 a.m. My movement woke Roy and he asked me what was wrong.

"I can't believe it but I've wet the bed."

"Your water must have broken. You don't have a history of bed wetting. We knew it would be soon. Are you having any pain?"

"No."

"Good, we've got a long time then. Go back to sleep. It's too early to get up. It will be hours yet." With that he turned over and was soon snoring.

Sleep. Who could sleep now? I was having a baby soon. When would the pain start? How bad will it be? How can he sleep at a time like this? Doesn't he know that I might have questions ... that I might be afraid?

I lay in our double bed - on the wet spot - with eyes as big as my belly for four more hours before he awoke. I still had no pain. After he ate his usual bowl of cereal he called the obstetrician who told us to come on to St Vincent's Hospital.

Dr. Edwin Waldrop had a needle inserted in my arm to cause the contractions to start. While waiting for the medicine to take effect

I was cold, so I covered up. No one could see that the needle had come out of the vein and the medicine was forming a large pouch under the skin. I had no contractions and didn't dilate. Later, when they found the mistake the doctor ordered an x-ray.

"It's a placenta previa," Dr. Waldrop told Roy and then explained to me, "That means the baby can't come out the normal way. The placenta is blocking the birth canal. I'll make an incision in your lower abdomen to deliver the baby. You won't feel a thing."

I was prepared for a normal delivery but not for an operation. I remembered my surgery for appendicitis. I was sick before and after the operation and thought I would never again be able to stand up straight, due to the pain.

Now, I was so scared. I didn't know it could happen but my knees actually knocked together. They didn't stop shaking until the spinal block paralyzed me from the waist down. I was awake but the area was draped so I couldn't see anything except Roy standing beside me.

"Don't cut. I still have feelings. I'm not dead yet."

"We don't use that term in the operating room," Dr. Waldrop said.

A little after 5 p.m. the baby we called "Thumper" was born. Roy Franklin Roddam Jr. was born April 28, 1967. To avoid having two Roys, we had decided to call him Ricky if it was a boy.

At last I could eat; I hadn't all day. I slept a good bit in the next hours before I started vomiting. I couldn't keep anything down. The next day I was so weak I couldn't lift my head. I just turned it toward the side of the bed to try to vomit on the floor but it went into my long hair. I couldn't answer the phone or have visitors. I seemed I had tubes going everywhere and they planned to run one down my throat to my stomach.

"Please, Roy, don't let them do it," I begged. "I can't stand anything else."

Roy took my hand and with tears in his eyes prayed, "Please, God, make her well. If you will let her live I promise that we will tithe from now on."

But, we didn't even attend church.

Promises made in dark times are often forgotten in the sunshine, but Roy kept his word. I stopped vomiting. I didn't need the stomach tube. We began to tithe by mail.

God also helped Blythe Gabriel of Waynesville, NC. He was diagnosed in 2017 with Merkel cell carcinoma in his left leg, a rare form of cancer of the skin which can spread to other parts of the body and become very hard to treat. It spread to his lymph cells in his leg.

Shortly after the diagnosis, Blythe was at his church in Waynesville, N.C. when he felt a cool breeze blow across him, without there being any fan or open window. He saw something like a hand over his right groin area.

Then he heard God speak, "Blythe, you are healed," before he saw that human form go out through the wall.

Ten days later he had surgery to remove all the lymph nodes in his right groin.

His physician told him the next day, "I don't know why I operated on you. There was no cancer there."

Five PET scans during the last year and a half has validated the same fact that he is cancer free. Blythe is married to Briarwood church member, Regina Phillips Gabriel.

With a head full of black hair and brown eyes, our baby, Ricky, looked just like his father. I thought he was the prettiest baby I had ever seen. Mama said every black bird thinks her babies are the blackest.

We brought our son home to a brick, ranch style house on Willow Brook Lane in Vestavia Hills where we had moved the week before he was born. He had his own room, right across from ours. He slept in a mesh-sided playpen with the bottom raised to crib height.

A slight noise awoke me when Ricky was about two months old. I was breast feeding so I was always alert for his wanting to nurse.

"Roy, come quick," I screamed. "Ricky is hanging in his bed!"

He was caught by his chin. His body had slipped down between the mesh side, the mattress and pressed wood floor of the playpen. Hanging there he was unable to cry. While I supported him from underneath, Roy threw out the mattress. We couldn't free him by pulling him up or pushing him down. People think it is fear that gives you extra strength, but it is actually God. Roy was able to free Ricky by tearing a hole in the pressed wood board. It was impossible but he did it. The next day Roy couldn't rip the wood at all. Those playpens were later taken off the market due to infant deaths. But the Lord had spared our son.

Eighteen months later, Melissa Renee was born on September 30, 1968. It's an old wives' tale that you can't get pregnant while you are nursing. Again, we had another beautiful, c-section baby, a clone of my husband. It seemed none of my genes showed up in our children and I was glad. While nursing Renee I became pregnant again. So much for having to adopt!

Four months into this third pregnancy, blood and tissue showed up in the commode. Roy said I probably had a miscarriage. Unconcerned, he didn't tell me to call my doctor. The next day I asked him, "Do you think I should call Dr. Waldrop?"

"Yes," he said. "I was wondering when you were going to do that."

Duh. Dr. Waldrop told me to report to the hospital immediately.

The next month I had a period. Since I didn't have periods while I was nursing this was only the second one since our marriage. Then, I had no more, I was pregnant again.

Lord, you can stop answering that prayer. My cup overflows.

With two toddlers I had less time for myself, especially as they got more and more control of their bodies. Interested in everything, they were making plans for the future. First, they were limited to things at floor level. To keep them out of the lower kitchen cabinets I hung rubber gloves over the doors. It make it look like monsters were trying to claw their way out. Or so they thought. The children were only mildly psychologically scarred. I had to be creative to keep them out of drawers and doors and places they shouldn't be. There were no baby proof items then.

Once while my father and I built shelves in the garage, I let Ricky play on the patio which was between two adjacent exterior walls - the den's and the garage's. Each had a door to the patio. Renee was napping. Ricky loved playing in the water. So to entertain him, I turned on the hose, letting him fill the toy swimming pool on the patio. I could look out from the garage and see him. I was holding the board while my father nailed up supports when I noticed I didn't hear the water running. Ricky was not on the patio. Even at his young age, he apparently could tell I needed help cleaning the house. So he pulled the hose into the den to wash down the sofa, tables and the television set. I dried the wood furniture with towels but the sofa and the shag carpet had to be pulled outside to dry in the sunshine.

Another day as I sat in the den sorting laundry, Ricky disappeared from the den. Then, I heard a splash from the bathroom. He was helping again. He had emptied the bathroom trash can into the commode. His father's shoes were on the floor, and he threw those in also. Luckily, I got there before he flushed.

"No. No. We don't throw Daddy's shoes into the toilet. And Mommy empties the trash into the garbage can." I closed the bathroom door. "I know you were just trying to help Mommy. I'll let you help me clean the den after I give Renee a bath." Ricky followed me as I carried Renee to the kitchen to bathe her in the sink.

While I was busy with Renee, Ricky disappeared into the den and started cleaning without me. He 'polished' the den furniture with almost the entire bottle of Brute after shave lotion. It was either the silence or the smell that got my attention. I was able to get most of it off before it turned the tables completely white. On the den shag carpet the lotion acted like bleach, creating a kind of polka dot pattern.

I should have learned to check on them when it became calm and peaceful. For some reason, the children were always quiet when they were up to something. I guess I was just thankful they weren't arguing over some toy, trying to drown out each other or crying over some hurt. It gave me a short break or a minute to finish whatever task I was doing without interruptions.

But when I didn't get angry, cry or scream over their actions, I laughed.

Whenever I vacuumed, their crying would interrupt me. They didn't like the sound of the Electro Lux vacuum so I told them, "Don't be afraid of it. The vacuum does a very important job. Mommy uses it to get up dirt."

As I was dressing, I heard the vacuum in the den. When I got there Ricky and Renee were busily helping again - this time getting up dirt. Using the vacuum's hose they had sucked up lots of the soil from around the roots of our five foot tall rubber tree. Later, they 'fertilized' it with dry, automatic dish washing detergent. The rubber tree finally died from all their care.

When Renee got diaper rash I let her run around without a diaper to help her heal, while keeping her corralled on the kitchen's linoleum floor by blocking the doors to the carpeted rooms. When she urinated I mopped it up. But when she did more than that, I got it up with toilet paper and took it to the bathroom toilet. While I was gone she dropped some more. Ricky had been watching and always my little helper, he got the mop and smeared it everywhere. He had seen me mopping up the urine so I couldn't be mad at him. I threw the mop away and wished I could have done the same with the kitchen flooring. But I had to clean up that stinky mess.

When a neighbor came over, Ricky told her Renee had "dodoed on the floor." After the neighbor left I told told him, "It's not polite to say 'dodo' in front of other people."

He asked me, "Do you say it behind them?"

Ricky also tried helping others. Somehow he got the gas cap off his grandfather's car and then filled it up with water from the hose. A wrecker had to pull the car to a repair shop so the gas tank could be taken off and drained.

Renee wasn't innocent either. Roy's father drove a Birmingham transit bus to the Billy Graham Crusade at Legion Field and he let Renee ride with him. Grandpa let her play with the controls and pretend to drive. Then, after everyone boarded the bus, Grandpa started the engine but the bus wouldn't move. He tried everything, but nothing worked. The parking lot was almost empty when another driver came to help and found that someone had engaged the emergency stop button on the floor.

While watching me put on makeup, Renee asked me why I wore lipstick.

"To make me pretty," I told her.

She must have wanted to be beautiful because later she put it on her lips, face, head, hands, body, legs and even her bottom. It took several baths to get all that beauty off.

I was folding several loads of clothes and diapers while watching TV. Ricky was playing at my feet and I thought Renee was taking a nap. But she had awakened and went into the bathroom adjoining our bedroom. She climbed up on the commode so she could turn on the water in the sink. Then, she joined us in the den. I continued folding clothes. As I carried the clothes down the hall to the bedrooms, I was met by an approaching stream of water. Renee had left the water running in the stopped up sink. It overflowed, came out of the bathroom, soaking the wall-to-wall carpet in the master bedroom before advancing down the hall towards the den. We couldn't dry our carpet so it soured, mildewed and smelled. It had to be replaced.

While I was cooking dinner, Ricky and Renee were sitting at their little table in the den, making pictures. By the time I noticed they were missing they had made pictures on both side of the the walls of the15 foot long hall with pencils, crayons and magic markers. It wasn't a pretty sight on the walls or of their mother screaming.

When playing marriage Renee told Ricky the vows, "Do you take this woman to be your awful wedded wife?" I wondered if her Daddy told her that.

Is this the life I always wanted? Cleaning the house, cleaning the walls, cleaning the clothes, cleaning the dishes, cleaning bottoms ... cleaning, cleaning, cleaning. I never knew children were so messy. It never ends. The demolition squad is right behind me. Then it's to do it all over again.

I guess I thought they would be like my dolls.- staying where I put them and not creating more work for me. I could not have been more wrong. But now I could understand why some animals eat their young.

Chapter 10

I WANTED THE children to go to kindergarten so I would have the mornings free for about six weeks until the new baby arrived.

We picked a Montessori school which allowed the children to learn by "spontaneous activity in a prepared environment rather than by direct instruction," according to their literature. This would allow the three to six year old child to become 'normalized' and be characterized by "spontaneous discipline, continuous happy work, and sound sentiments of help and sympathy for others." I was all for that.

Rick, three and a half, and Renee, two, began the Montessori Creative Preschool in 1970. It was the first time they they had been left without me and they cried until I was out of sight, I was told. I guess that's when they began the "continuous happy work."

We learned from the progress reports that Renee seemed to adapt or become more normalized than Ricky.

One report said, "Ricky gets along with other children ... but occasionally he enjoys fighting with the other boys and girls. His social awareness is keen but hindered because some of the children are afraid of him. He wants the attention of his peers. But when he doesn't get what he feels is his share of something, he resorts to small harassments of the children."

As I thought of the other children at school, I was the one developing "sentiments of help and sympathy" - for them.

I went to the hospital the night before my scheduled cesarean section for our third child. "Once a cesarean, always a cesarean" was the medical directive at the time. At two o'clock the nurse brought me a baby to feed. But mine hadn't been delivered yet.

Our beautiful baby, John Randolph, was born at 8 a.m., October 16, 1970. My Catholic obstetrician asked if I would like a hysterectomy since my abdomen was already open and I heartily agreed. At last I was cured of constantly being pregnant and/or nursing. Without that I'm sure I would have lived like women did in my grandmothers' day, having a new baby about every two years. Nursing must make it harder to conceive, even if it doesn't prevent it.

With a new baby I had even less time to watch the other two. I still had two children in cloth diapers so I washed diapers almost daily.

Every day started the same. I'd get up early to get a cup of coffee and hopefully sneak outside for a quick smoke before they woke up. But, children do not sleep late until they turn six and enter the first grade. As they age it becomes increasingly harder to wake them. By the time they are teenagers, you have to literally drag them out of bed.

But now they were like roosters, up making loud noises at dawn and ready for the first fights of the day. I prepared breakfast and refereed the table disputes. After cleaning up the spills and the dishes, I dressed them.

I hoped for a little time alone for a bath. But if the door was closed and locked, they beat on the door.

"Mommy, Mommy. Come fast," came the little voice from the other side of the door.

"What is it? Is everything o.k.? What do you need?"

"If you don't hurry it will be too late."

"What happened?" But there was no further comments from outside the door. I was out of the tub instantly and wrapping a towel around me I ran dripping to the den.

"What's wrong? Who is hurt?"

"Oh, you are too late. You should have come sooner. It's gone now."

"What's gone? What's the emergency?"

"I wanted you to get me that space gun that was on TV."

After that I just continued to soak when they beat on the door, tattling or sounding like they were killing each other. Only when there was a prolonged silence did I rush from the tub to see what they were doing.

The children weren't acting like I wanted them to behave. They took up all my time. The drudgery of having three preschool children was overwhelming. I had no help and no time off. Soon I was experiencing my usual depression that I'd had off and on since I was a teenager.

It was hard to keep things clean and neat. When I caught Rick throwing paper on the floor, I said, "If everyone threw their trash down, our house would look like a pig pen."

"No," he said. "It would look like your car."

Even my children recognized I had a problem keeping things clean.

There was less to clean up when they played outside. So in the summer if it was as hot inside as outside, they would play in the fenced, shaded backyard. We lived as Roy and I did when we were children with the windows open and no air conditioning. I wore shorts with as little as possible. Roy gladly left for work after breakfast and a cooling shower. He didn't fuss about the heat; he liked saving money by having a lower electric bill, plus he usually wasn't there during the heat of the day. When he got home he stripped down to his underwear. That was fine when it was just the family, but as the children got older their little friends started coming to the house.

"You probably better start wearing some shorts," I told Roy.

He agreed. But every night he continued to sit around in his underwear. Early one evening he was in the den reading a newspaper when Renee came in with a little girl. Luckily, Roy had the newspaper to hide under.

"Roy, you've got to remember to put on shorts. You don't want to be caught again in your underwear by a little child or worse, a parent."

He nodded and grunted, but I didn't know if he heard me or not. He had the male ability to look straight at you and appear to be listening but never hearing a thing. Or at least it never registered. Later, we learned to say, "Earth to Dad. Earth to Dad" to make sure we had his attention.

It wasn't long before the same thing happened again. He came into the den in his underwear.

"Come on children. Come with me." I took the children back to the bathroom and stripped them down to their underwear. Then, I stripped down to mine. We all went back, sat down in the den. Roy looked up from the newspaper and noticed the children in their underwear. Then, he did a double take as he saw me in my bra and panties. That cured him; he never sat around in his underwear again.

Randy came up with his own solution for being hot. We had been to Gadsden to a July family reunion and were driving back to Birmingham. All the car windows were down and the children had taken off their shirts to cool off in the back seat. Air conditioned cars didn't become universal until some time later. People were smiling or even laughing as they passed us. Finally, I turned around to see why. Randy was lying on the rear window's shelf above the back seat, completely nude.

We wanted the children to experience everything. We took them everywhere when they were very young. By the time they could understand and enjoy the outing, we were tired of taking fussy children to all those places.

At four and a half Rick went to his first football game. When he got home Renee was very interested. "Did you really go to a football game?"

"Yes."

"Did you play football?"

"No, they wouldn't let me," Rick said. "They had guards to keep the people away."

"What did you do?"

"Nothing. I just sat there with all the people they wouldn't let play. It was boring."

I could understand. That's the way I always felt about football.

When we took them to the zoo they liked looking at the animals. When I pointed out the deer's horns, Rick asked, "How does he play them?"

They also liked the animal exhibits at the Alabama State Fair as well as the kiddie rides, and cotton candy. Baby rabbits were for sale. After much begging, promises and crying on their part, we bought a cute little black and white bunny. He just cost $5. He was a sweet pet and allowed the children to drag him around and feed him ice cream. He liked to lie on his back and have his stomach rubbed. But after a month he became listless. Did he have too much ice cream? I didn't know if ice cream was good for rabbits. The rabbit was sick and not getting any better.

"You better take the rabbit to the vet," Roy told me. "We don't want the children to see it die."

The veterinarian was able to keep him alive for two more weeks. He ran up a vet bill of $85 before he died. So much for a cheap pet.

Roy grew up attending Camp Winnataska, near Birmingham. Over the years he was a camper, a leader and finally a "Blackfoot," a teenage worker who did construction work, took care of the animals and generally ran the camp. One night as he settled down in his sleeping bag he felt something crawling up his leg. Immediately, he knew it was a snake. His blood curdling scream accompanied his rocket exit from his sleeping bag. The laughter of his friend, Ted Teague, revealed who was responsible for the prank. Other friendships formed there with Jim Thorington, Fletcher Yielding and Bob Russell lasted long after their camping days ended.

When Ricky was three months old Roy worked as assistant

director of the Chicos, the younger boys' camp at Winnataska. As a child I never knew camps existed, but on seeing the first snake, near where I was walking, I knew it wasn't for me. If there is anything I hate, it's snakes. Thereafter, I refused to leave our cabin without Roy. But I did enjoy having a week of not having to cook or clean.

Roy wanted to expose our children to his beloved camping experience so each summer we continued going. If Roy wasn't a director, he was the camp doctor. The first two or three summers Rick got very little out of it except a lot of attention. But the fourth year he enjoyed making messes, 'swimming' twice a day and best of all, being his Dad's shadow.

Renee and Randy also went as toddlers and would have been happy anywhere they were fed, changed and allowed to do exactly as they wanted. By the time they were old enough to go as campers Ricky and Randy decided they didn't like the regimented activities. Only Renee grew to love spending time there each summer.

During my childhood we drove by Silver Springs several times on the way to see relatives in Plant City, Florida. I always begged to go into the park, so my parents would stop. But when they found out the cost, they drove on. I was so disappointed. They said it was just too expensive.

Taking our own children to Disney World, we stopped at Silver Springs. When Roy heard the price, just like my parents he said, "We're not going in there. It's costs too much."

I didn't want to relive my childhood; I wanted to see those glass bottom boats. "Oh, yes we are," I insisted. "I've wanted to go in there for years. It's not too expensive to keep peace in the family." Roy recognized the truth in that. We all enjoyed it. It was worth every penny, especially to me.

One activity we hoped would help train the children was Bible Club. It was held weekly at our house with Carol Thomas from Briarwood Presbyterian Church teaching the book of Exodus.

One attendee, a five year old neighborhood boy, came in one week with very muddy shoes. He tracked across the kitchen floor.

Then he lifted his foot and raked the mud off his shoe onto the wallpaper at the corner of the wall between the kitchen and den. Then he did the same thing with his other shoe. We all watched with our mouths open but Rick acted. He walked over and socked him in the nose, knocking him to the floor. That's when we saw our own exodus as the crying boy with the bloody nose ran for home. The other children started leaving too. Soon, there was just us and Mrs. Thomas and she was getting her things together. I couldn't punish Rick. If he hadn't done it, I might have. It seemed we learned very little from the lessons in Exodus about obeying God and leaving our sin nature behind.

"I guess he is getting his sleigh ready," Rick said to his father.
"Yes, I guess so."
"I'm trying to figure out if he is real or fake."
"Why do you think he is a fake?"
"Well, last year everything he brought had price tags on it."
"Maybe Santa had to buy some of the presents."
"Oh, Dad, what do you think the elves do."
When I heard about this talk I knew why the price tags were there. I knew that was one busy elf, who had decorated the tree and the house, planned, bought the food and cooked the Christmas dinner. After making a list of the presents for everyone, shopping to get the best prices, and then buying them, she was tired and forgetful when she wrapped them late at night, after everyone else was in bed.

Ricky was growing up. At six he rebelled against wearing the cute, matching outfits that he, Renee and Randy wore. He insisted on wearing only blue jeans and a white undershirt as he started first grade. An angel, named Mrs. Stropp, his teacher, rewarded Rick by having him put a sticker on a chart when he wore a regular shirt to school. She credited his positive attitude for his progress in all areas including social behavior. She said it was easy to work with him.

That was the year he changed his name. After six years of calling him "Rick or Ricky" he told us, "That's not my name. I want to be called Roy."

It sure was hard calling him by his given name but eventually all of us did, except Roy's father who continued to call him Rick or Woozie. Now we had a big Roy and a little Roy.

Chapter 11

WHILE THE CHILDREN were in elementary school a patient gave us a Shih Tzu puppy. Told it was a Chinese dog, Little Roy asked, "Does he bark in Chinese?"

Since they had a battery operated toy dog they wanted to know if this was a real dog or just a toy.

This breed of dog needed its hair brushed every day. On some days I didn't have time to brush Renee's hair, much less a dog's. One day in my busyness I failed to watch the puppy. He got outside, ran into the street and was hit by a car. Due to the resulting blindness, he had to be put to sleep.

We loved our home on the corner of Willow Brook and Linda Vista Lanes in the Gentilly Forest neighborhood. Unfortunately, it was on a direct route to Berry High School. Teenage drivers frequently flew down our streets.

Early one evening when I was cooking, I wasn't watching Randy and he got outside. I didn't miss him until I heard the squealing of the tires. Randy, as a toddler, had run out between two parked cars into the street.

The teenage boy, with his head down on the steering wheel and his eyes closed, asked, "Did I hit him?"

"Car hit me," Randy said for a long time afterwards. It apparently brushed against him but he wasn't injured. Again God had intervened in our life. This time by saving our youngest son.

It should have never happened. How could I let my baby almost get hit by a car? I was worried more about the meal than watching the children.

Roy wasn't concerned with my mothering abilities. In his new job as director of Medical Education for the Baptist Hospitals, Roy was under pressure to set up a residency program for Princeton and Montclair Hospitals. At home Roy prepared lectures or studied for his upcoming board certification in Internal Medicine. All that preparation did pay off. He passed the board exam on his first try.

"Those teenagers are driving too fast when they go by our house," I told Roy. "I'm going to talk to the neighbors and see how they feel about having a speed bump installed."

Since I lived on a corner I talked to all the neighbors on the front and side streets of our house. Everyone agreed that it was a good idea. Someone suggested we have it installed right above our driveway which was on the side of our house. There at the entrance to another subdivision were big, brick pillows on both sides of Linda Vista Lane. Nobody would be able to drive on the grass to bypass the speed bump. Cars would have to slow down.

Shortly after it was installed, a six by eight foot sign went up in the yard diagonally across from our driveway. Located in that adjacent subdivision. It said, "Dr. Roy Roddam 822-5334 is responsible for this speed breaker. Notice it doesn't affect him."

We began getting all kinds of calls - complaining, harassing or obscene - at all times of the day and night. When we began getting threats I called the police. The flowers I had planted around our mailbox were pulled up and our yard was trenched. I wanted to retaliate but I didn't know who was to blame for the vandalism. A good guess was the teenage boys who lived in the house with the sign.

As a child I got in numerous fights. I always wanted to get even with those who crossed me - first my brother, then those in high school and now these people. My negligence in not talking to them about the speed bump was not intentional. We placed the speed breaker there so cars couldn't go around it.

"We can't let this continue," Roy told me one night.

"You are right. I feel the same way. But what can we do, since we aren't actually sure who is causing all the mischief. But it's probably those boys that put up the sign."

"That's not what I mean," Roy said. "I'm not talking about getting even. We have to go and apologize to them."

"What? Apologize? Never! They should apologize to us. We're just trying to protect our children."

"We have to do what's right whether they do or not. We didn't consult them and they are the ones who have to drive across it."

"You can go, but not me. I'll never go. They are in the wrong, not us." I stuck out my lip. I was getting angry at him for taking their side.

"We are both going and if they want it removed, we will have it removed."

I hated knocking on their door. Roy introduced us and then apologized to these people, my enemies. I still didn't think we were as much in the wrong as they were. I wish I could say they were gracious and accepted our apology but it didn't happen. Roy sounded like he was truly sorry. I was just there because he made me go. When Roy offered to have the speed bump removed, they said they would take down the sign.

Roy was always trying to teach me how to live and treat others. Even if I went in kicking and screaming like a child when confronted, eventually I saw he was right ... but it often took years.

Roy wasn't perfect. Who is? I certainly wasn't. He did have that most important characteristic - he was a Christian and acted like one.

Janet Edwards also helped her non-Christian mate. (Names have been changed.) Although her husband, Jack, was unfaithful Janet chose to stay in the marriage and pray for her husband to be saved. As a protestant Janet had promised when they married, to raise their children in the Catholic Church.

"As a Christian I was attending Bible Fellowship, where I noticed Briarwood members had a different life style. I was beating Jack over the head with scripture and praying God would change him. The Lord revealed to me that I needed to be changed, too."

Jack agree to visit Briarwood where they found the pastor's sermons were different from what they were used to hearing. On one of their initial visits they ran into Richard Condrey, Jack's friend and fellow employee at IBM. He invited them to Sunday School, where the message spoke to Jack so much that he wanted to go back again. They joined Briarwood and Richard, who had been praying for Jack, discipled him.

Janet's prayer for her husband had been answered. Shortly after Jack had to take early retirement due to a heart problem. Then seizures revealed he had a brain tumor.

"This brain tumor is nothing," Jack said, "I know where I'm going." He died seven months later in 1989.

"Our children got to see the changes in their father after he became a Christian," Janet said. "It made me thankful for the hard times because that's when God draws us closer to him and his faithfulness."

Richard Condrey knew God had saved him from death in 1943 in order to be used by Him.

As a Navy midshipman, Richard was to fly to Virginia from his Navy airbase in Texas for amphibious training. Most would be flying on Navy DC3s but some would be traveling on Navy C119s. A friend, who had crashed on two of those C119 type planes in Korea, said he was never going to fly on one of those again.

The next morning Richard and that friend were ordered to get aboard a C119.

They obeyed but Richard was told to get off. Half the men, scheduled to fly, had been delayed and Richard would take the next flight with them on a DC3.

"When we landed in Virginia," Richard said, "we were told to call home and tell our folks we were o.k. since one of the C119 planes had crashed on takeoff. My friend, who had warned me about those planes, was on the crashed plane but managed to get off. He was the only man that got off alive. He reentered the burning plane to try to drag out his buddies. They all died, including my friend."

As Randy grew he followed his siblings, exploring their world as they destroyed mine. Randy loved to 'write' on everything: paper, books, TV screen, floors, walls, furniture. When he found an ink cartridge that fit in his Dad's fountain pen Randy did as he always did with everything, he put it in his mouth. The squishy stuff wasn't that good so he spit it out on the rug in his Dad's office. It's surprising how much ink there is in a tiny canister. Another wall to wall carpet ruined beyond repair.

Randy imitated everything his brother and sister did and even his Dad. Roy frequently swung his golf club inside to practice. One of Roy's swings broke the ceiling fan light. So he couldn't say much when Randy swung a golf club hitting and destroying our television screen. We soon had to buy another TV when Randy destroyed mother's picture tube with his BB gun.

Are other people's children like ours? I never heard that they were. But then, I sure didn't tell anyone about our children's actions. I didn't know to ask the Lord to help me with my reaction. Nor did I know it was wrong to seek to get even with people. Consciously or unconsciously, I tried to get even with Roy for my perceived slights. Now, my children were also my combatants.

Roy always hit golf balls or worked out at the gym before coming home. He said it was to avoid the afternoon traffic. On the weekends he had standing golf games and in the afternoons he watched sports on television with the door to his office closed so he could enjoy the shows.

"I never have any time off," I once complained to my father. "Roy never lets me have any time to be away from the children."

"You leave him alone." Daddy took his side. "He needs time to recover from making life and death decisions. He's got to have time to relax."

When do I get some time to relax? Of course, I'm just a housewife. But I was making life-long decisions too, about how our children would turn out. Child rearing was left to me. As Erma Brombeck said, "The role of the father is just a bit part - a walk on."

I wondered if other husbands helped around the house or with the children, but I didn't ask. I wouldn't complain to Roy. He was having problems with some egotistical doctors at the Baptist hospitals. I couldn't add to his problems.

I sure wasn't very attractive. I was frazzled in looks and attitude when he got home. I was too tired or angry to welcome him. I was hungry to feel love and acceptance. But I felt he just wasn't there. He seemed like my mother - unavailable. He was rarely home and when he was he escaped to his office. We met in bed when I wasn't too tired. I wish someone had told me then, what a prominent lady Bible teacher said, "Never say no to your husband, after all it only takes about five minutes."

I had expected to live "happily ever after," but I found out children were not like my dolls. Children are messy, disruptive, tiring and disobedient. When I put them in bed they didn't stay there. When I cleaned them up, they just got dirty again. When I told them what to do, they ignored me. I wasn't prepared for all the work that was my responsibility. Children hadn't changed Roy's life but it sure did mine. Every day was the same as the day before. The only free time I had was when they napped and then I usually napped too.

Even though I wanted to blame Roy I knew it was really my fault. I felt like a failure at my job. I just wasn't a good mother. I was easily upset. Although I was messy, I couldn't stand their making messes for me to clean up. Although I was angry, I went ballistic when they were not kind or gentle. Nobody told me children are self-centered and I didn't recognize that it was my own self-centeredness that cause all my reactions. I couldn't stand their screaming at each other so I screamed to correct them.

I was basically lazy, so I hated their not putting away their toys and didn't want their 'help' because it just created more work for me.

Most of this I didn't recognize in myself. I just knew things were not right in our family. Since I was responsible for the children, it was my fault.

We started to church because I thought religion might help but it didn't improve the children's actions or mine. Maybe, I was not quite as quick tempered, but we still had bedlam at our house. My father told me once, "Somebody has to be in charge, but it's still a toss up here."

In their own way the children tried to rule over me. Mothers are so used to managing children so it is easy to also try to manage husbands. At least, it was with me and that created conflict. But the real reason was I didn't want to be in submission to my husband as the Bible teaches.

Is this all there is? I have everything I have ever wanted and prayed for but I am so tired, so unhappy, so angry. It's not what I expected.

Life is a mixture of happiness and sadness. You can't choose what happens to you but you can choose your reaction - either to laugh or cry. I wish I had known that. But at the time their antics just made me angry. They weren't amusing tales to share. I kept them secret because I thought they reflected by poor mothering abilities. I felt I wasn't a good wife either. Then, with my father's heart attack and subsequent death and the suicide of a childhood friend, my depression sank to the suicide level. Only God's 'letter' saved me and started my pursuit of knowing Him through Bible studies.

But I had a long way to go.

Chapter 12

AFTER THE TROUBLE with the neighbor over the speed breaker, we decided to move away from the dangerous streets and build a house in the Tanglewood section of Vestavia Hills. I drew up the plans with ideas from magazine clippings I had saved for years. The first floor had a living room, dining room, den, master bedroom, Renee's bedroom, laundry, two and a half bathrooms plus an office for Roy, an art studio for me, and a playroom for the children. Upstairs were two bedrooms, a bath and an unfinished area which was later developed into a guest bedroom. Every bedroom had a walk-in closet.

The dining room had a 12 foot long built-in cabinet with shelves for tablecloths, place mats and napkins and other serving pieces. The tile top was useful for serving. In the foyer was a sky light, a glass shelved display cabinet for Roy's chess set collection and a recirculating fountain which ran down the back side of the living room fireplace.

But, it was a good thing we took my plans to an architect for review because I forgot to include a place for the furnace and hot water heater. I didn't want any wasted space.

A year before we moved we got a new dog. Tiger, a large ginger colored, shepherd type dog, showed up at Roy's parents. No one knew who he belonged to and no one advertised for him, so they brought him to us. While moving into our new house, we didn't notice that Tiger disappeared. But later that day, one of our new neighbors, three houses away, came to tell us that our dog had attacked their small dog and put him in the hospital. What a way to be introduced to the new neighborhood. We paid the vet bill for their dog's week-long hospital stay.

As new construction, our house didn't have a fenced yard. It did have a walled courtyard with a gate, so that became the dog's outside dog pen.

Three weeks later the neighborhood children were over playing hide and seek with our children. Someone left the courtyard gate open and Tiger promptly went up the street and put the same dog back in the hospital again.

"The dog is leaving today or I am," I told the family. "I don't care which."

Roy took our dog to his aunt's in north Jefferson country. Boy, did I hate facing that new neighbor again. The Rhodes' family pet had only been back home a short time from the last attack. They were gracious when I told them that we no longer had a dog. Again, we paid the vet bills. Soon they got another dog, a new puppy ... a breed noted for its fighting ability.

A couple of years later a stray mutt showed up at our house. Of course, we fed him, loved on him and he stayed around over a week.

"Can we keep him? Please let us keep him," the children begged. There were no newspaper notices or neighborhood signs for this lost dog, so Roy agreed the dog could stay.

"Better take him to the vet and get him checked out and up on his shots," he advised.

Dogs never like going to the vet. This dog must not have really been mad; after we brought him back to our house, he left that night, never to be seen again. I wish he'd gone home before we spent $80 at the vet's.

Later, my brother gave us a new puppy, a white ball of fur that was the offspring of his two small dogs. I tried to make him stay in the playroom area. As I prepared dinner, I would allow Rolf to remain in the open doorway between the playroom and kitchen. He would lie there, but whenever we were not looking, he inched forward a little by little until he was completely in the kitchen. The dog thought we wouldn't notice. But he was so cute. In no time he had the run of the whole house. If you gave him an inch, he'd take a mile.

Rolf loved to destroy squeak toys, which made a sound like a distressed ground squirrel. He would not stop biting and chewing the toy until it stopped making that noise. One day I had Rolf in the car with me when I stopped at a garage sale. I bought him a new squeak toy and squeaked it a couple of times. He went crazy wanting it. I put it in the glove compartment. I had to stop at the grocery store so I did not give it to him; I didn't want to pick up all the pieces of the toy in the car. When I returned to the car Rolf had tried to get to the toy. He had chewed off all the padding on the dashboard down to the metal and the pieces were everywhere. It was destroyed. Roy was not happy.

Rolf grew into a medium size, Poodle looking dog. Although he didn't fight with other dogs, Rolf didn't like strangers, even if they were nice to him. Once we had couples over to play bridge. One of the men, Tom Leopard, rubbed Rolf's back, scratched his ears and even gave him a dog biscuit. But as he left that evening, Rolf bit him on his shoe. Thankfully, it wasn't his leg.

I learned that a dog's negative behavior is caused by poor training by their owner. Dogs need limits on what they are allowed to do. I couldn't train children, so I don't know why I thought I could teach a dog.

Probably because I fed him, he became my dog, and he was determined that Big Roy would not have a higher rank in the pack. He frequently growled at my husband.

"What are you doing?" Roy would ask the dog, "Don't you know I buy your dog food?"

"Roy, you can't reason with a dog."

Our dog, like our children, didn't obey. You can try to instill right thinking with the latter but it must be by your actions, which they copy, not by your words. The Bible warns us, as well as the secular teaching, that actions speak louder than words.

Judy Bishop, my former college roommate, had an uncle with a cabin on the Gulf of Mexico between Panama City and Destin, Florida. The sugar white sand and turquoise water beckoned you to stay on and on in that idyllic place. When the house next to her uncle's went on the market, my roommate and her brother snapped it up. When we went to see it, I told Judy's mother, "If another one of these houses is ever for sale, please let me know."

I love Florida but Roy hated the sand and insisted we were not going to the beach the next summer.

Then we got the call from Judy's mother. "The house next door to Judy's is for sale," Mrs. Hinton said. "If you are interested you need to come right away. The owner, Mrs. Washburn, has not listed it with a real estate agent yet."

I ran to tell Roy the news.

With interest rates over 20% on home loans, Roy told me, "I don't know if we can afford to take on another house payment." This was during the Carter presidency.

"We can at least look."

Roy, as head of the household, had the final say whenever there was a decision to be made. I could argue all I wanted, but eventually he made the decision. Even though this is what the Bible teaches it took a long time for me to accept it. I fought this principle until I learned that submission doesn't mean inferiority; we are equal with mutual cooperation. The wife should submit to her husband by choice as Jesus submitted to the Father' plans. Also with the authority Roy then had the whole responsibility for the outcome.

Without even seeing it, I really wanted that house next to Judy's on the beach. We agreed we would leave it up to God. We were trying to live as Christians. We prayed, asking the Lord that if we were supposed to buy it, there would be no problems or glitches.

If there were, then we would know we were not to assume all that debt.

We went down to see the house the following weekend.

A childless couple from Chicago had built the four room, concrete block cottage in the 1960s when the husband retired. He died several years later. His widow, Mrs. Washburn, didn't mind living alone in this sparsely populated stretch of beach as long as the two ladies lived next door in the house that Judy bought. But the winter after they sold and moved away was too much isolation for Mrs. Washburn.

Her house had a large living room, kitchen and eating area, a large bedroom, one bath, another room which was used as a laundry and an attached garage. But the best part was the 50 feet right on the the Gulf of Mexico.

When Mrs. Washburn told us the cost of the house, it was the same amount that Judy and her brother paid for their house next door.

"We like your home, and Roy thinks it would probably be a good investment," I told her, "but that's what the house next door sold for, and it has four bedrooms, three baths and was sold furnished. We feel like $70,000 would be a fairer price."

She thought about it for a minute and then said, "I think you are right. I'll take that price."

We later learned that a man was waiting for us to leave so he could offer her more money for the house, regardless of what we were willing to pay. But, we had an agreement with Mrs. Washburn. We got financing, and Mrs. Washburn quickly found a house to buy in Panama City, closer to friends and medical care. No glitches. I felt that God had given it to us.

The laundry room became our bedroom with a double bed. We put three sets of bunk beds in the large bedroom for the children and their friends.

We loved the almost deserted beach, located about 20 miles west of Panama City and 20 miles east of Destin. There was nothing between our cluster of cottages and the three dozen or so houses at Sea Grove Beach, about a mile away. We could leave the world behind, and no one could reach us because we never had a phone installed. Roy could really get away from the hospital and patients.

We learned about the beach and the fish by experience. I was terrified of stepping on a crab, so I wore tennis shoes in the ocean. I wish I had thought to made and sell shoes to wear in the water, as someone did later.

When we took some of Renee's little friends to Florida with us, the sea was full of small fish. To let the girls catch them, we tied fish hooks to string and used niblet corn for bait. They caught a sand bucket full of the small Pompano. Roy cleaned them, and I cooked them, not knowing there were rules about the size of fish you can keep.

Another time, we fished from the boardwalk along the bridge on Highway 331 over Choctawhatchee Bay. At dusk we began catching fish that growled at us when we caught them. Not recognizing the fish, we asked some nearby women if they were edible. They assured us that those fish were good eating. Although the fish had a lot of bones, we cooked and enjoyed them. Later, when I told Judy Bishop about it she said they were trash fish, and nobody she knew ate them.

Driving to Panama City we kept seeing signs promising several different kinds of submarines on Thomas Drive. We decided to take the children to see the submarine museum. We followed the signs until we reached the location. But the children weren't educated about submarines; we were. It was a restaurant, selling eight different kinds of sandwiches called submarines.

A friend, Neil Haskew, told us about a discovery her husband, Doug, made on the beach at Sea Grove in 1954. Doug saw a piece of metal sticking up in the sand, began to dig it out and discovered the body of an Air Force pilot still strapped in his ejection seat. The young man had been missing eight days. The family had just received his metals posthumously the day before his body was discovered. God had his body found for closure for his family.

The world didn't find our part of the beach until Seaside was built in 1981. Until then, everything at the beach was closed between Labor Day and Memorial Day with few exceptions.

So when Renee, Randy and I went down to the beach the fall after Renee got her driver's license, the beach was pretty much deserted that weekend. Renee and Randy had to return to Birmingham for school that week. They would return the next weekend with Big Roy and Little Roy. I didn't mind being left alone. With no one to look after, I could spend all day painting beach and ocean scenes.

"Get all the money out of my purse," I told Renee. "You'll need it to buy gas and a meal on the way home. I've got everything I need here" I waved them off and sat on the patio enjoying the deserted beach.

The next day I arose to a dreary, rainy day. But it didn't interfere with my painting at the kitchen table. When I stopped for lunch, I noticed the wind was whipping around the palm trees next door and shaking the windows. The ocean was gray with big waves breaking as far out as you could see. Usually the ocean lapped the shore like a big lake with little or no waves. I had never seen it so rough. And the rain was increasing in volume. I turned on the television.

Everyone from Apalachicola to Fort Walton Beach, which included our area, was ordered to evacuate due to an approaching hurricane. It was expected to hit somewhere in the northwest panhandle, probably the next day.

Then, I realized that I couldn't evacuate; I had no car. No one was staying in any of the nearby houses. With no telephone I couldn't call anyone. I had no money to catch a bus over on the highway. I only had a bicycle. I could just see myself soaked, cold and fighting to see, as I peddled my bike out in the pouring rain and whipping wind down our shell drive to highway 30-A, then state road 395 and finally onto U.S. highway 331 North. Would someone stop and offer me a ride?

God, you have to help me. I don't know what to do. There's no one to help.

I closed and fastened the sturdy shutters on the outside of the windows. Inside I debated whether to put on dry clothes when someone knocked on the door.

"We wondered if anyone was here."

There stood my cousin, Linda Barkley, who lived in Gadsden, Al. She told me that she and her husband, Mick, had to cut short their vacation in Panama City Beach. They came by our beach house on a whim to see if anyone was here. But I knew it was the answer to my prayer. God sent them to bring me out of that situation.

On the way home I stopped and called Roy. He was walking out the door to come and get me. He knew I had no way to get home or call him.

The former owner had told us about staying alone in this house during a hurricane. She said she would never do it again, although only the garage was blown away. This time we had no real damage at the beach house, another gift from above.

Other hurricanes washed away the stairs to the beach several times and kept eroding our front lawn. One caused about $10,000 damage when it knocked out a window, damaging the floor and drapes which had to be replaced. In the front rooms every surface, even the vertical ones, were coated with sludge-like sand and debris.

Initially Hurricane Michael in 2018 was headed straight for our beach house. But instead it turned to the right and came ashore about 40 miles away at Mexico Beach, which was destroyed. We had no damage.

Chapter 13

I WONDERED IF I was truly a Christian. I really hadn't changed that much. I still flew off when the children reflected my bad behavior, self-centeredness, or anger. The only thing I noticed was that I no longer cursed. I didn't frequently curse, but on occasion a bad word would slip out.

I knew I needed to eliminate all bad talk, when Ricky grabbed four year old Renee's pillow and she said, "Give it to me, damn it."

But it was not a conscious action on my part; the Lord just took it away. I wished he would do the same for my desire to smoke.

When I started smoking the risks were not widely known. It was a way to cover my shyness and lack of conversational skills. I didn't want the children to smoke so I knew it was time to stop. I had tried several times before, only to start again when I had to have a cigarette and bought a pack.

This time I had a plan. I took a pack of Winston's across the street to a neighbor's who smoked. If I had to have a cigarette I would go to her house but I wouldn't have others at home to smoke. I went over twice, in the six months before the battle was won. She continued to smoke and died with a heart attack some years later.

I avoided people who smoked. In times of greatest desire, I would eat mints or chew gum. I gave up the things that I associated with smoking, such as coffee. And I promised myself that when the children left home I could smoke again.

And this time I prayed for the Lord to help me get over this addiction. It was the hardest thing I ever did and I only succeeded because my prayer was answered.

"Jo Anne, can you come to a spend-the-night party at the lake next weekend?" Susan Huff asked. She told me that the women, who would be there, were the ones in that first Bible study, I attended after God intervened in my planned suicide. Many of them had also joined our church.

I paused. I'd never heard of married women having spend-the-night parties. That was an activity where teenage girls talked about boys, clothes, and girls not there, while doing each others nails and hair.

"What would we do?" I asked.

"Oh, it's to play bridge and to give us a little break from the usual routine."

I did need a break. Roy agreed I could go. We played bridge and as in high school, the 'girls' did nails and hair, too. But they didn't talk about people who weren't there. They talked about themselves.

They also prayed. I thought people only prayed at church or at a Bible study.

Even though they were strange, I had a good time. So when asked, I joined their monthly bridge club. And, that spend-the-night party evolved over the years to extended weekend trips out of town with the group.

The Lord knew I needed examples of Christian living. We do become like the people we are around. That's why it was so important to have strong Christians as friends. Listening as they prayed aloud, seeing how they served the Lord and others, and hearing about the answers to their prayers built my faith.

C.S. Lewis said about friendship, "The next best thing to being wise oneself is to live in a circle of those who are."

Some moved away and others joined, but all were united in

Christ. Our bridge club is like no other group I have ever been in. I felt their love and laughed with them about their escapades. I saw how they handled their children and responded to their husbands. They are there for each other during the good and the hard times. Proverbs 17:17 says "A friend loves at all times ...".

Although we were not all of the same denomination we were bonded together by our faith in Christ and in serving Him and others as directed by the Holy Spirit. While their actions were usually consistent with their words, on occasions we cautioned or corrected each other.

Gossip is hard to resist. In a Bible study the pastor said that sharing derogatory secrets about another person, even if true, becomes gossip when you are not part of the problem or the solution. Therefore sharing that information should not be used as a pretext to ask for prayer for someone.

As a Christian I had to be trustworthy. I improved, but I wasn't always successful. My old nature still had the desire to pull others down to what I thought was my level. The bridge club, without realizing it, mentored me. This allowed the Holy Spirit to begin to change me.

One night before Roy retired to his home office he told me about a patient, a young woman who had been brought in unconscious that day.

"I can't find any cause for her condition. There's no evidence of trauma, infection, cancer or poisons," he told me. "I gave her a variety of tests. Maybe the results will give us a clue."

Nothing changed the next day or on the days to come as more of the test results didn't give answers about her condition or how to wake her up. I had the bridge club praying for her as Roy and I were doing.

Twelve weeks after her admission Roy told me, "The family wants me to remove her feeding tube. She would eventually die."

"Are you going to do that?"

"No, I can't. I don't know what is wrong with her, nor what her prognosis is, but I can't let her be starved. That's what I told the family."

God wasn't ready for her to die. She began to improve. Eventually, alert and talking, she was discharged from the hospital in a wheelchair. Later she completely recovered, married and became a mother. The reason for her unconscious state was never discovered.

Shortly after this episode, Roy returned to UAB to teach in the medical school while seeing patients in the UAB clinic. God had given him the ability to solve mysteries like Sherlock Holmes, but Roy's were medical puzzles. From a through history and physical he made the diagnosis and treatment plan.

He became quite comfortable with his routine, occasionally not paying attention to the questions he asked patients. For instance, to one he queried, "And how old were you when you were born?" Another time he asked the diabetic, "Do you check your urine in your sugar?"

But there could also be misunderstanding on the part of the patient. Once when a woman was getting a pelvic exam with her feet in the 'stirrups', the lamp being used to illuminate the vaginal area would not stay correctly positioned.

Frustrated with readjusting the lamp to get it to illuminate the area, the doctor commented to his nurse, "It looks like this thing is worn out."

"But, Doctor," the patient said, "you don't know the life I've led." She didn't recognize that he was talking about the lamp.

When Roy was examining an elderly woman she told him, "When you are young your body gets you in trouble, but when you are old, your body ain't nothing but trouble."

All those hours spent studying in his office resulted in his having many "pearls" to give the students about different diseases. They appreciated his preparation by choosing him as Best Teacher three times and Best Clinical Professor once. He was promoted to full professor in 1978.

God is the ultimate source of all honors we receive. The Bible says we must not take credit for these but acknowledge that God is the source of any of our successes. Otherwise we are in danger of becoming proud. Proverbs 16:18 says, "Pride goes before destruction, a haughty spirit before a fall."

In medicine or in his hobbies of golf and bridge, Roy never forgets a thing he's learned. But in other areas, he sometimes either doesn't remember or just doesn't pay attention, truly acting like the absent minded professor.

Once when Roy borrowed his father's truck, he stopped to fill it up before returning it. After pumping the gas, he replaced the gas nozzle on the pump and the put the gas cap back on. Then, he drove off ... without paying.

The gas station attendant got the tag number and in a few days the sheriff came to arrest Roy's father for stealing the gas. He denied doing it. When told the date, he knew that was the time his son had his truck. Roy was thinking about something else that day.

The police almost got Roy another time. He went to Belk's to pick up some pants that had been altered. As he was leaving the men's department he saw an Alabama jacket which he tried on but decided not to purchase. As he exited the building a loud ringing occurred. He didn't know what it was. He looked around but didn't see any reason for the sound. When he got to the car he found he had somehow gotten the Alabama jacket underneath the plastic clothes bag holding his pants. He carried the unpaid for jacket back through the door and that same ringing occurred again. He didn't know expensive clothes had a devise attached to them that had to be removed or an alarm would sound as they exited the building. No one came over or said anything to him this time either, so he took it back to the rack and hung it up.

Another time when Roy and I played in a bridge tournament and were exiting out the door, Roy said, "Just wait here. I'll get the car and pick you up."

In a few minutes I saw him pass by the building. At the corner he turned onto another street and drove out of sight. I figured he was replaying the bridge hands in his head and would think about me in a minute and return. Some time later he did return. He said he didn't notice that I wasn't in the car until he got home.

Roy has always been hot natured and didn't need much cover but I wanted a warm bed so we got an electric blanket with dual controls. We left the blanket on year round. Each fall I would get down both dual controls from the top of the closet. One fall we had an early cold snap. As I got ready for bed, I noticed the electric blanket on his side was plugged in.

"Where is my blanket control?" I asked Roy.

"It's still in the top of the closet."

"Why?"

"I didn't get yours down."

While he took his shower I sat on the bed stewing that he didn't think of me. Then, I thought of a solution. I just unplugged the control from his side of the blanket and plugged it into my side.

As he was getting in bed he said, "What are you smiling about?"

"Oh, I'm just so happy." *And warm,* I thought.

Another year when it was bitter cold I switched on both controls and set them on medium. When Roy got in bed I still wasn't warm enough so I turned up my control a couple of notches. When it didn't get warmer I turned it up some more. Still nothing. In frustration I turned it up to high. But if anything it was colder.

"I think this blanket has stopped working."

"Stopped working," Roy said, "You must really be cold natured. I've been cutting this thing down and I'm still sweating. I've turned it off."

Then it dawned on me. I had switched the controls. I was adjusting his side of the bed and he was adjusting mine.

Chapter 14

AFTER DADDY'S DEATH, Mother decided to move to Gadsden so my grandmother, who now lived with her, would be near her other children who could then help in caring for her.

To get rid of unneeded items before she moved, mother and I planned a garage sale, although neither of us had ever been to one. She was selling lots of green glassware which I didn't want. It had been given away at movie theaters or included in cereal or other boxes of food during the 30s. We sold it for 25 cents an item. Not long after our sale I visited my first antique shop and saw that Mother's green depression glass was selling for $12 for each piece.

She asked me if I wanted my scrapbook of movie star photographs. In the 40s and 50s you could write to celebrities and they would send you a signed picture. All of them sent the free pictures, except Marilyn Monroe who sent a price list. I wrote a letter to Bing Crosby, asking some questions and received his answers back in a signed letter from him along with his publicity photo. I regret that I threw away that scrapbook.

Daddy had a large barrel of metal cuts, which are metal illustrations used on the printing press. At the sale a man asked how much we wanted for them.

"What do you want with those?" I asked.

"Oh, I'll find a use," he said.

We sold the barrel containing at least a 100 cuts for two dollars. I saw that man at every antique or craft show for years afterwards selling each one mounted on a wood block to act as a stamp for $2 each.

I decided I would start going to garage sales because there must be others, like me, selling their good stuff at junk prices.

Garage sales spoil you for shopping in stores. At one estate sale I found two boxes of Victorian, glass, figural Christmas ornaments for $1 a box. There were houses, birds, fruits, Santa Clauses, musical instruments and other shaped ornaments. That started my collecting old Christmas decorations, especially old Santa Clauses. Frequently a young, attractive, female lawyer beat me to the old decorations. Pete Partin owned a Christmas shop in addition to working as a attorney. Years later we became good friends when we competed again, this time at duplicate bridge.

At a yard sale I found my good china, Engagement by Royal Worcester. It had been discontinued and was no longer available in stores. The mother of the woman selling my china had died and left her daughter two other complete sets of dishes. So she didn't need the seven place settings plus extra cups, saucers, salad plates and bread and butter plates in my pattern. She had reduced the price for all of that from $75 to $50, the price of one place setting when it was available in stores.

If you wait long enough you can get almost anything at a garage sales. That's where I got books, toys, games, clothes, jewelry, small appliances and some antique furniture for the living room. But Roy wasn't happy with the drop in our checking account.

"Jo Anne, you are just spending too much money at garage sales. I could understand if you were writing checks to grocery or drug stores."

So I started writing the check stubs for my garage sale items to John Smith's Grocery or Paul Brown's Pharmacy.

When Roy told me I was writing too many checks, I began to use the credit card and got cash back. When he complained about the credit card bill, I went back to writing checks. I wasn't working at the time and had no other way to support to my growing addiction which eventually led to my having the pack rat syndrome.

I did get rid of some things I purchased from others at my own garage sales. At one, because sales were slow, I told my daughter we needed to have red light special.

"No," she said, "that would be a blue light. Red lights are not used to draw in customers at this kind of business."

I got my husband interested in garage sales by taking Roy to one that had something he liked. If you can't beat 'em, get them to join you. We were in Chicago at his medical meeting. In a rental car with a city map, I navigated two freeways to get to this estate sale. I decided to return the next day when everything would be half price. Roy's meeting was over, so on Sunday he went back with me and discovered 12 golf putters at $1 each and golf books and other hardback books for only fifty cents each. We had to buy two large suitcases at the sale to take all our purchases back home on the airplane. This was before you were restricted on the number of bags or their weight. It was a good thing. With the books the bags could barely be lifted.

I had also discovered flea markets and thrift stores and loved hunting for treasures there. Roy began buying things there too. But, sometimes those purchases were an embarrassment.

At a thrift store Roy found a tie with a pattern depicting the kidney system in a schematic drawing. No one but a doctor would have recognized it. He wore it to a medical dinner and was seated next to a doctor whose speciality was kidneys. He loved the tie and raved on and then asked Roy where he bought it.

"At a thrift store," Roy answered.

Silence. The other doctor was at a loss for words. He must have never known a physician that shopped in thrift stores and didn't know what to say.

Another time at a thrift outlet Roy bought a very comfortable pair of shoes with crepe soles. He wore the shoes to help a relative get a tread mill she was borrowing. The exercise device was on the second floor in the banker's upscale house so they had to struggle to bring it down the steps. At the bottom of the stairs the banker's wife looked back up and said, "What's that mess all over the stairs?"

Everyone looked and saw some kind of rubbery material on the steps. The relative was so embarrassed when she realized it was from Roy's shoes. The crepe soles had disintegrated until there were no soles left. They were on the stairs.

You have to really be careful what you buy. People sometimes have a reason for getting rid of their stuff. Our clothing continued to create problems.

I wore a new warm-up outfit to the church to do some errands. After an hour or so traipsing around and talking with several people in different offices, one of the ministers told me I had a tag on the back of my pants. I wouldn't have cared if the big stick-on tag spread across my fanny had said anything but "extra large".

Before a party at Vestavia Country Club I tried on everything in my closet - some long, some short - trying to find the right dress. At the party we stood around talking for a couple of hours until I had to go to the ladies room. As I walked by the full length mirror I saw that the final dress I had selected was floor length but had a split up one side which went up past my knee. Through the slit I saw my hose stopped mid calf.

I learned I could "correct" my clothes by coloring them. I've painted white buttons with pink or red nail polish so they would match the color of the blouse.

I found that black magic markers make scuffs, worn areas and spots on belts, purses and shoes disappear. Once I had a pair of tan shoes that I decided would be more useful if they were black so I painted them with a black marker. They looked great. But the first time I wore them in the rain the black color began to wash off. That time I had mistakenly used a marker that wasn't permanent.

I also used black markers to add details on print blouses so they would match the black pants I usually wear. But I should have known not to do this when I was sleepy. I went to sleep, while applying the permanent marker and ended up with a big black blob on a new shirt.

Subconsciously, I must have remembered hearing about my Dad's eating a hot dog for lunch and getting a spot of mustard on his white shirt. Returning to the News he tried to wash out the yellow stain but it remained. He solved it in the art department by painting the stain with white paint.

Paint can really freshen up things around the house. I colored small appliances black to match appliances and other things in the kitchen.

When the plants in a big half barrel planter on the front porch stopped blooming I got a small fir tree but it soon died too. I gave up on live plants and painted the fir tree with three shades of green spray paint. The paint held it together so it would not shed and the variations of color made it life-like. It lasted a long time until Roy Jr. and a friend discovered it was painted and began picking off parts of the plant each time they walked past it.

It's so hard to buy gifts for men. They rarely get anything interesting, just ties, socks, shirts, and boring things like that. One Christmas, among other things, I gave Roy a new, white, dress shirt. After the holidays it was laying on our bedroom dresser, still in its plastic wrapper. I put it away on a shelf on Roy's side of the closet, where it was forgotten.

Before the next Christmas I saw it and thought, *There's that shirt. I bet he'd never even know if he got it again.* So I wrapped it up.

He was pleased. "I can always use a new, white shirt," he said.

Again he didn't wear it or even open it, so eventually it went back in the closet once more. That started a trend. Each Christmas I wrapped up that shirt. The children and I laughed as he unwrapped the same shirt, year after year. Whether the gift was so boring or so indistinguishable, he never remembered having gotten the shirt before. We finally told him. I saved a lot of money on Christmas gifts for him.

But, he paid me back. He may have remembered my birthday but he forgot to shop for my present until that afternoon, when he was either playing golf or hitting golf balls. So with no time to shop anywhere else, my present came from the golf shop. Every year I got all kind of golf items - golf earrings, a golf shirt, a golf skirt, a golf jacket, golf book or something with the golf or club logo on it. He loves golf so much he thought anyone would be happy with those gifts. But I don't play golf. Finally, I told him he'd better make sure the next birthday gift I got wasn't about golf or for his birthday he would be getting an expensive piece of jewelry, made for a woman.

I also tried to save money by searching grocery ads for the best prices so I would know where to shop that week. I clipped and cashed coupons when I remembered to take them with me to the store.

Once I tried to save by giving myself a home permanent. At a garage sale I bought the beauty shop rods, used to roll the hair for a perm.

"Roy, could you help me give myself a perm?"

"I can't do that."

I knew what to say. "You would save yourself over $50."

"Well, I guess I can try."

I washed my hair and rolled it up with the tissue paper on its rod. Now Roy was to squeeze on the permanent solution. But there was no pungent odor as he was applying it. He had picked up the neutral-izer which stops the curling action, instead of the permanent solution sitting beside it.

I had to start over - wash my hair, roll it up with the papers on the rods and then have Roy put on the permanent solution. After the required time, the remaining neutralizer was put on. I never tried that again. Permanents only give you curls for about three months. Roy said that was a misnomer - it was anything but permanent.

Sandy Wheeler, told the bridge club how she 'saved' money. Her father-in-law, who lived out-of-town, was always bragging about how little he paid for certain groceries, as he checked out those in her pantry. She got tired of it so when she got a new jar of peanut butter or mayonnaise or such, she just replaced the lid of the new purchase with the one from the old jar, which usually reflected a cheaper price. By the next time he came for a visit she had replaced the lids several times. He was amazed at the prices she was paying. She was finding "better deals" so he stopped bragging about what he paid for items.

Roy tried to help me save calories and not gain weight when he brought home a big bag of Hershey's Kisses that a patient had given him. "That's wonderful," I said. "I want some."

"No. You're on a diet."

No matter how much I begged he was determined. He wouldn't let me have any. When he went to work the next day I searched for the candy. He had it well hidden in his office, but I found it. I turned the unopened package over and used a razor blade to cut it open under the overlap. Then, I ate all the chocolate I wanted, saving each piece's foil and flag. By trial and error I got bits of newspaper inside the silver paper and twisted the top with the Kisses strip sticking out. I replaced these in the candy bag and used double stick scotch tape to seal the bag underneath the fold. Then I hid it back where it had been.

Several days later when I got home from shopping Roy was in a tizzy.

"Jo Anne, you won't believe it, but someone at the Hershey candy factory is eating the candy and then stuffing their foil wrappers with newspaper pieces and including them with the real candy. I'm calling the factory ...."

I burst out laughing so hard I couldn't say anything.

"You did it," he said. "I don't know how, but you did it."

There was a mix up when Lon Evans' grandfather was in charge of building a wooden crate for clothes his church was sending to an orphanage in China. After the box was packed, the carpenter missed his glasses and realized they must have fallen out of his shirt pocket into the crate and were now on the way to China. He was so angry because he had just spent $20 to get them, which was a lot of money during the depression.

Months later the director of the orphanage was in the United States thanking the congregation for their gifts to support him.

"I was so thankful for everything you sent but for one thing especially. The authorities in the country, where I serve, took my glasses and destroyed them. I couldn't read without them - the Bible, correspondences or anything.

"But when I opened your shipment there was a pair of glasses - the exact ones I needed. It was as though they had been custom made for me."

The people in the church listened, happy for the miraculous glasses, but confused because they hadn't sent any glasses.

Sitting quietly in the back, with tears rolling down his cheeks, Lon Evans' grandfather knew the Master Carpenter had used him in an amazing way.

Chapter 15

REV. FRANK BARKER has a heart for the lost so he taught his flock how to share their faith. Then, they would train others to do the same. On Wednesday nights after a short class, teams of three members - a trainer and two trainees - would visit the homes of church visitors or people new to the community.

I felt Roy would be a natural for this. It was easy for him to learn, he enjoyed speaking with people and his job gave him a platform to be able to talk with his patients about spiritual matters. But he was resistant. So I signed up. I would get him involved later.

I misunderstood and attended the first week which was for trainers. Trainees, like me, were to come the next week. Dr. Barker had an appointment to visit a family and asked if I wanted to go with him and one of the trainers.

After small talk at a church visitor's house Frank explained the significance of Christ's death and resurrection and what it means to believe. The couple knelt and asked Christ into their lives. I thought, *if only I could learn to do that.*

That unspoken prayer was answered. On the way back to the church Rev. Barker said he had gone through his "Longer Presentation" so I could hear it. That meant I could memorize it and give that wonderful explanation just like he had.

But it was not easy to learn Frank's "Longer Presentation" so the church switched to Evangelism Explosion, a gospel presentation by Dr. James Kennedy of Coral Ridge Presbyterian Church in Florida. It contained five points, which could be amplified with scriptures and illustrations. We didn't convert anyone; that was up to the Holy Spirit. If the person asked Christ to be their Savior and Lord, they were then told how they could grow in the Christian walk.

Roy did get involved, and we both took trainees out on visitation for years. But while I saw the Holy Spirit use me to lead some people to pray to become Christians, Roy saw three times as many.

A lot were his patients. After addressing their medical condition, he would seek permission to ask them two personal questions: "Have you reached the point in your spiritual life where you know for certain that when you die you will go to heaven?" This question was to determine if they had assurance of salvation. The second question was "if you did die and God asked why He should let you into His heaven, what would you say?" This question was to determine what he/she was depending on for their salvation. Based on their answers as prospects, he would share the good news after asking and receiving their permission.

Occasionally, someone would object. Roy was called on the carpet by three different superiors at the University Hospital and told to stop witnessing. His faith gave him the courage to obey God, not man, so he continued. The Lord moved all three of those men out of the University but Roy remained. He was tenured and unlikely to be fired if he asked and was given permission to shave his faith.

Under the leadership of Rev. Dan Allison, Evangelism Explosion Director, I shared too. Teams of three went to the homes of Briarwood visitors, new residents or knocked on doors to do a questionnaire, in order to present the Gospel. One night, a young lady that prayed to receive Christ, told Rev. Barker and his team she was planning to commit suicide that night, before they visited and gave her hope.

Rev. Bruce Stallings, Executive Pastor at Briarwood Presbyterian Church, told about an experience he had. A woman, who lived out of state, called him and said, "My unmarried daughter, who lives in Birmingham is planning on having an abortion.

Her name is Elizabeth Anne Green (not her real name). Would you talk to her and try to stop it. She wouldn't listen to me. We are estranged so I don't have her address."

Bruce wondered how that mother could think he could find this unknown, young woman, with that little information, living somewhere in Birmingham.

Later that week at a restaurant the server's name tag said, Liz. Being short for Elizabeth, Rev. Stallings thought that it was interesting that this girl had that name.

He was prompted by the Holy Spirit to ask, "Are you Elizabeth Anne Green?".

"How did you know my name?"

Instead of answering that question, Bruce asked, "Are you planning on getting an abortion?"

"How did you know that?" she asked

"Your mother called me. She loves you, God loves you and He wants you to keep your baby."

Rev. Stallings told her why God loved her and what He did to save her from eternal separation from Him. The young lady began to cry, prayed to receive Christ and decided not to destroy her child.

Another night while doing questionnaires we saw two Mormon girls speaking to a man at his apartment door. We asked if he would mind answering two questions but he didn't speak English so the Mormons translated into Spanish for us. Based on his works answer, we told him God's plan of salvation, all of which was translated by the two Mormon girls. God can use anyone - even those who don't understand God's plan of salvation themselves. That's what happened that night when they translated into Spanish for us and that man became a Christian.

On the day I visited a new eye doctor, I asked him what he would tell God about why he should be in admitted to heaven. He said "because I am about helping other people."

When I asked him if he would like to know what the Bible teaches about how to have eternal life, he said he was comfortable with his position and felt that it was inappropriate to talk about such matters now, when he needed to be focusing on his job of correcting my sight problems.

Knowing his 'sight' was the greater problem and my imperative was to warn him, I said, "I understand your position and I certainly want you to focus on my eyes, but we never know what lies just around the corner. I may not have another chance to share with you and probably never in a non-medical situaatioin. This morning my daily Bible reading was in Ezekiel 3:18-21 where God says if we don't warn sinners their blood will be on our hands. I don't mean to offend you but if I have to choose, I'd rather it be you than God. But if you prefer, I'll just send you a note containing what I wanted to say."

In the letter I told him that his good deeds would never be good enough because his sin would always keep him out of heaven. If he wanted to go to heaven based on his goodness he needed a perfect record with no sins because only the sinless would be admitted. Since God is holy, which means without sin, He can have nothing to do with sinful men. So how do we get in? Jesus, who lived that perfect, sinless life, paid the price for our sins on the cross when He died and arose to offer us admittance into heaven. We can secure this gift not by just head knowledge about Jesus or by trusting in Him for temporary emergencies, but by believing in or trusting in what He did on the cross to save us for all eternity and not trusting in anything else. That is saving faith.

But first we must admit that we were not really saved when we were trusting in our own good deeds to save us. Our record is what we need saving from. We need to pray, asking Jesus to be our Savior and Lord and admitting that we can not save ourself based on what we have done.

I explained that I was also sending the track that was helpful for the minister who founded Briarwood Presbyterian Church. I explained that Frank Barker, Jr. thought he was a Christian because he believed Christianity was true, that Jesus was who He said He was and because he wasn't too bad. He did not understand that faith was not just believing but also trusting in Him for salvation. Even ministers can misunderstand that you are saved by grace alone, through faith alone in Christ alone.

I pray the Holy Spirit worked in the eye doctor's heart.

We inherited Roy's father's old Chevy truck. It broke down at the corner of Action Road and Old Rocky Ridge. A man in his late 30s stopped and helped Roy push it into a parking lot there. They determined all the oil had been thrown out, since the oil cap was missing. The stranger said he would go get oil for the truck. Roy didn't give him any money to pay for it. Roy called me to come so he could go and get oil if the stranger didn't return. When I got there it had been awhile so Roy told me to wait in the truck and he would take my car and go get some oil.

While Roy was gone the young man showed up with the oil, a funnel and an oil cap. I wondered why this had happened so I asked the two evangelism questions. He gave the right answers but said he stopped believing in God a long time ago.

"I still believed He existed, but I wasn't living for Him and had not for years. Then, I got into some real trouble," he told me.

"Why do you think that happened?" I asked him.

"Maybe, God was trying to get my attention.

"I think you are right. Did it get your attention?"

"Yes."

"Well, what are you going to do about it?"

"I suppose I need to get back to God."

"Yes. But how do you do that? Where do you learn about God?"

"In church."

"But be sure it is a church that teaches that all the Bible is true. Not one that picks and chooses which parts to believe. You need to attend a church like ours."

"Where is that?"

"Right here. Right up the hill from where we are standing. At the top of the hill go right or left to the front of the church where there is a visitors parking lot. Why don't you meet us there for church tomorrow?"

"I will."

"Good. We'll meet you in the foyer of the church at 8 a.m. tomorrow. How much do I owe you for the things you bought for us?"

He handed me the register receipt for $40 but I only had $20 so I told him I would give him the other $20 at church tomorrow. Although, over the years, many people have told me they would meet me at church, they never did. He did show up with his wife, got his $20 and stayed for church. But he never returned.

Owing money and repaying them at church is one way to be sure they will visit at least once.

I carry a little change purse that has my driver's license, main credit card and a couple of zippered areas for money. It also has a coil to hold my keys.

I was in Winn Dixie shopping and as I checked out, my change purse was not in the grocery cart. Without it I couldn't pay for the groceries and anyone who found it could use my credit card. Without the keys I couldn't drive or even unlock the car. Plus, in it was a good bit of cash.

I thought, *I really do need a keeper. I can't even go to the grocery store without messing up. What am I to do?*

I prayed, *"Father, please help me find my change purse. I know it was due to my carelessness, but you control all things, so help me find it and I'll try to learn from this."*

Then, I retraced my steps. In the produce section the grocery clerk saw me searching and asked, "Is this what you are looking for?"

He was holding my change purse. I was so thankful. But why did it happen?

The Lord told me in my heart, what I was to do.

David, the grocery clerk, thought he would be going to heaven but he didn't know why God should let him in. When I explained he prayed to receive the free gift of salvation. David now is certain of the entrance requirements and that he meets them.

And now, I understood why I lost my change purse.

Antonio Andrade, as a young, unmarried man, left Mexico with his father and two brothers to work in Rainsville, Al. One night at their rental house three masked men with guns broke in, demanded money and then opened fire. Antonio saw that one man was aiming at his head. At the last moment Antonio put his arm up and the bullet hit him near his elbow. His father was shot in the stomach. The only one of his brothers who was present was killed.

"I felt so guilty for living. I wanted to die, too," Antonio said. "I had a Catholic background but I had never been interested in spiritual matters."

A cousin, who had asked Christ into his life, had been urging the rest of the family to read their Bible and become Christians. That just made Antonio angry.

"But when this happened, I wanted to know why," Antonio said. "I started reading the Bible to find the answer and I fell in love with it. When I read the gospels about Jesus and his life, I invited Christ to be my Savior and Lord. God had me live so I, and many more of my family, could someday live with Him in Heaven."

My daughter was having work done in her house and wanted me to be there while the workers were in the house. That first day the only workman who spoke English prayed to receive Christ. I decided that when I went back the next day I would get him to translate into Spanish for me, if any others gave the wrong answer.

But he wasn't there that day.

One of the other men spoke a little English. When he did not understand he had an application on his phone that allowed the English spoken into his phone to be repeated back in Spanish. I was amazed. I'd never seen anything like it. I just spoke God's plan of salvation into his phone and it spoke it back in Spanish.

God provided in advance for that man and one other, who was listening, to both become Christians.

Sharing the gospel is not a gift; it is a command.

Chapter 16

PART OF ROY'S job at the University was to lecture to the residents, interns and medical students. One day he invited me to visit one of his classes.

"You've never heard me lecture," Roy said, "why don't you come down today. I'm speaking on hirsutism."

"What's that?" I asked.

"Women who have excessive hair, especially on their face."

I decided to go and went by a costume shop on the way. I sat on the second row. All the medical students were clustered in the back of the room, rows behind me. After nodding to me, Roy launched into his lecture about hairy women. I reached in my purse and put on the mustache I had purchased.

The lecture went on and on but Roy never looked at me again. He was speaking to the students. When Roy met me outside the hall I was wearing the mustache.

For a while, soon after we had joined Briarwood, I took refreshments on Sunday nights for the youth. Once when April Fools Day hit on a Sunday, I prepared special snacks. I took Oreo cookies and scraped out the sweet filling, replacing it with white toothpaste which looked the same. I enjoyed watching the teens reactions as they tasted the cookies. Some teenagers would bite into a cookie and then look for a place to spit it out without anyone seeing. When they started making faces and commenting on the taste, I reminded them it was April Fools Day and brought out the good cookies.

At another church function I was asked to provide four dozen cookies. I decided to try to make diet cookies, so I substituted saccharin for the sugar. Mistake. They tasted awful. I didn't have time to make four more dozen, so I topped them with a sweet butter cream icing. I watched people bite into my cookies. As the sugar hits their taste buds, they never acted like they tasted the bitterness underneath.

When Renee's in-laws were coming to visit I made a new, supposedly, fabulous Surprise Chocolate Cake. When I poured the icing over the cake it didn't look right but I carried it to her anyway. It was a surprise all right. When I got home I found the sugar, I had failed to put in the icing. The ease of making the cake was suppose to be the surprise.

I think everyone has a responsibility to teach children's Sunday School classes. Having taught a couple of times before, I knew Roy was a great teacher. I began to prod him to teach again. I'd help by checking the roll, bringing goodies and planning parties.

"I'm doing all I can right now," he told me. "If you think it's our time to teach again, then you teach."

That week at Bible study, Dr. Barker taught the Hebrews 5:12 verse which says, "In fact, though by this time you ought to be teachers, you need someone to teach you the elementary truths of God's word ..." Dr. Barker then asked "How long will you have to keep going over the basics. When will it be your time to serve the church?"

I knew God was speaking to me.

I agreed to teach but began to have doubts about my ability, my knowledge and my time commitment. Also I couldn't read the Bible aloud because I had only been taught sight reading, not phonics, so I couldn't sound out all those proper names. But God is greater than our weaknesses. He just wants our availability. Because of the excellent teaching material, I didn't have to be concerned about my teaching skills or my Bible knowledge. Like everything else, you learn by practice. You learn to teach by teaching. I began teaching fourth grade girls.

The inability to pronounce names from the Bible was actually an asset. The little girls didn't mind reading aloud because they could read better than the teacher! Also, they saw that God could use anyone.

While teaching, I remembered how many Sundays my children went to Sunday school and church without eating breakfast. As many adult classes had coffee and donuts, I decided I would bring drink boxes and cup cakes in case the children had not had time to eat that morning. I arrived at church between 6:30 and 7 a.m. to set up my class before early church at 8 a.m. On each desk I put a napkin with the drink box and snack, the lesson sheets and a puzzle or two, appropriate to the lesson. If the girls had a puzzle to do, while waiting for the others to arrive, there was less bedlam.

I also had a prize box of assorted small gifts, earned by reciting memory verses or doing a random kindness. I encouraged them reach out to the girls they didn't know because if the children are not happy in Sunday school, the parents usually leave the church.

Because Briarwood has a school, where most of the children in Sunday School attend, those in public school were often left out and were not a part of the clique. I tried to prevent this in my Sunday school class. But even the adults do the same thing. It is just human nature to talk to friends instead of talking to unknown people. It's understandable, but it's not right. Those you don't know may be visitors or newer members who need to be included in conversations.

I remember Little Roy asking me once, "Do I have to go to rejection class?" Try as I might, I couldn't make my boys fit in at Briarwood. Several times we intended to leave Briarwood, but then God would have Roy elected a deacon or elder or asked to teach a class, so we would stay.

I fit in well with ten-year-old girls; we had the same interest - Barbie dolls. These dolls arrived in the early 1960s with their fashionable clothes. I had always loved dolls. And even at my age I thought it was fun to dress them.

That Sunday School hour was the most meaningful time of my week. I learned more than the students. God also used it to prepare those fourth graders to face serious situations. The mother of one of the girls died. Another student sustained a serious head injury at an amusement park. Fathers lost their jobs and parents threatened divorce.

One year we got a new girl in the class. Her family had recently left another denomination and joined Briarwood. Her Biblical knowledge was lacking, but she was a quick learner and soon, her hand was up to answer every question. Before they were promoted to the next grade, I would ask the girls to write down the answers to the two evangelism questions to find out if they were sure they were going to heaven and what they were depending on to get them there. This girl answered both correctly.

She was killed in a car wreck that fall. I knew she was in heaven.

Whether God uses lessons to give us faith, enhance our spiritual growth or help us face the hard times, we are taught his word does not return void.

I loved teaching the girls. If I had known how much fun it was to teach, I might have become a teacher. Children give you their love regardless of how you look, whether your mind is sharp that day or even if your actions leave a lot to be desired. And a child will give you a truthful answer.

One Sunday, after running down the hall because of an small emergency, which my husband handled, I arrived at the classroom winded.

"I'm sorry, girls," I apologized as I explained the circumstances. "I'm out of breath because I'm too fat to run like that."

"Oh no, Mrs. Roddam," one of the girls told me, "the reason why you can't run is not because you are fat. It's because you are so old."

I taught for 10 years. But I almost quit. I continued to struggle with depression, which can cause you to twist innocent remarks into criticism. It made me misinterpret a comment made to me about my Sunday School class. When I got home from church that Sunday, Roy read my face and asked, "What's wrong?"

"I'm giving up teaching." I said. "I'm driving the students away. Fewer and fewer come to class."

"That's not true," he said, trying to comfort me.

"No. I've made up my mind. I'm going to quit," I said. "If God really wants me to continue, I will. But He must show me by having someone express appreciation or compliment me on my teaching. And they have to do it before I leave town on Friday. You aren't to say a word to anyone."

I was putting out a fleece like Gideon did in Judges 6 to determine if God really wanted to use him to save Israel.

By Wednesday I hadn't gotten any messages about my teaching when Rev. Barker called to remind us about the Thursday night Bible study. Although Roy had a conflict, I decided to go alone, thinking I might get some help with my depression. Then, I smiled when I thought, *God wants me to go so someone will have a chance to talk to me about the Sunday School class.*

No, He wanted me to learn. In God's plan and control of events, the lesson at the Bible study was on determining God's will. I needed to hear all the instructions on how the Holy Spirit leads us. But it really got personal when someone asked about putting out a fleece.

The gist of the discussion was that this was an immature approach, made from a lack of faith.

"We don't use a fleece because now we have the Bible to tell us God's will for our lives, which Gideon didn't have," said Rev. Barker.

Then it hit me. God got me to the Bible study so He could answer me - but not in the way I had asked or expected. *God really wants me to teach.* I got the message and continued teaching.

Ten years later I quit. Ginny Catalano, who taught with me most of those years, continued teaching 4th grade girls for another ten years.

You'd think that anyone that got a 'letter' from God would live a changed life, but old feelings and habits are hard to break. I had evidence that God loved me, yet my default setting for most of my life was not feeling loved. I thought I didn't deserve love. You can't easily put off a lifetime of rejection, even if it is mainly self rejection. Real change take time and lots of it.

We normally go to early church but one Sunday we went to Sunday School and then church. Someone, I thought didn't like me, was so friendly I couldn't believe it. But when I heard the sermon I knew why. The message was on loving your enemies.

Just as the Lord had sent me a message, he also chose to assure Roy Sr. in a special way. Roy told me what happened.

It had been an uneventful day at the country club workout room when suddenly someone burst into the room shouting, "Come quickly! Someone is having a heart attack on the tennis courts."

Roy administered CPR while silently praying that God would spare the life of Briarwood member, John Sharpe. When the ambulance attendants arrived they did all they could, but Roy realized that John probably wasn't going to make it. Before going home Roy, visibly shaken, moved aside and began to cry as he prayed for John.

A few days later John's son called Roy and told him about a dream his father's tennis partner had. In the dream John told his friend, "Tell Roy I'm okay now and not to worry."

John's friend didn't know anyone named Roy and at first, John's son couldn't think of anyone either.

"But then I remember you had tried to help Dad on the tennis court," the son told my husband, "and I thought you'd like to know about the dream."

Although Roy realized it wasn't actually John speaking, he was grateful that the Lord used this special way to let him know about John.

Roy may not have been able to save John Shape's life but God used circumstances to stop Wales Goebel from his business of delivering whiskey and put him in the business of saving babies from death.

"If someone had been there to help, rather than condemn, maybe I would have had a baby, rather than an abortion." Wales Goebel heard a woman say.

He had believed for a long time that abortion was a result of lack of resources, education and support so he wanted to offer an alternate solution for an unwanted pregnancy. In 1980 Wales began Save-A-Life, dedicated to supporting the woman and sparing the child.

Thousands of babies have been saved. And if the mothers couldn't keep their babies, Wales established an adoption agency which could provide answers to the prayers of infertile couples.

Among other services are free pregnancy testing, ultrasounds, tests for sexually transmitted diseases, programs for fathers and childbirth and parenting classes.

Attending classes earns monetary credit to purchase items needed for the baby.

Chapter 17

OUR CHILDREN WERE now teenagers. I had wondered what they would be like after all their earlier 'helps'. I prayed that God would make them different from me. But frequently their reactions were just like mine. I should have known why.

Little Roy's seemed to have a chip on his shoulder, when he was younger. If a child looked at him like he was about to laugh, Little Roy might punch him even if he had never seen him before. So he grew up being a fighter.

He was as angry as I was, and this led to conflict and then to disobedience. It reached such a state that he told me he hated me and couldn't wait to get away from home. His father and I prayed that God would change his mind, never thinking how literally God would do that.

The tensions became so great in our house that we gave our oldest son the choice of going to military boarding school or living in our house under our rules. He chose to attend Marion Military Institute, a military preparatory high school and college about 80 miles south of Birmingham.

He attended his final two years of high school at Marion and thrived under the military regimentation. He was asked to join Swamp Fox, a high school and college organization known to have the most physically fit, disciplined, technically and tactically proficient members. They were required to maintain a 2.5 GPA and a 270 on the Army Physical Fitness test. His grades were now all As and Bs.

Until he got his car, he insisted on being picked up off campus because of the car we drove. The right car was important to him. He wanted his car to be a used BMW.

After graduating from the regimented, boarding high school Little Roy played, instead of studying, during his first year at the University of Alabama and his grades reflected it. He realized his poor academic record would keep him from being admitted to medical school. So he dropped out of the University to decide on a new major and enlisted in the National Guard. He went for basic training at Fort Jackson, South Carolina. There he won the High Physical Training Award for scoring the highest in push-ups, sit-ups and fastest time in the two mile run of any of the 500 men there. Next, he went to Fort Benning, Ga. to learn to parachute from airplanes as part of his Special Forces training.

Roy and I went to his graduation along with the wives or parents of the other men in his class. On the previous night's jump, one young man broke his leg. Now, three airplanes circled the field dropping off two parachutists on each pass. I've never seen so many women crying at one time, as we all watched, not knowing which parachutist was your loved one. The young men may have felt like crying when their parachute wings were pinned on their shirt. Without the metal backing behind the shirt, it pierced their skin when it was jammed through the cloth.

I was so thankful every time I heard he made another successful jump. It was a blessing not to know beforehand.

At Ft Lee, Virginia Roy Jr. learned how to pack parachutes. With basic training complete, he planned to go back to the university the next semester, which would be in the fall.

At Vestavia High School Renee was determined to get good grades. She never put off starting assignments and that, with other good study habits, resulted in excellent grades. She was inducted into the National Honor Society among other honors. Once she had decided to become a doctor, then, like her father, she was determined to do whatever it took to get into medical school.

My husband's education started with his being the pet of his first grade teacher, Vivian Slaton. After Roy and I married and had children, she saw Roy's photo in the newspaper and asked for us to be invited to her birthday party. She didn't drive, had never married and had outlived all her relatives. After the party the children and I began visiting her, driving her to appointments or running errands for her. Although there was about a 50 year difference in our ages, she and I became friends.

She introduced me to the Classics by loaning me her books to read. Then, when I returned a book, she'd tell me to keep it; she wasn't going to read it again. We included her in all our holiday celebrations and had her over for other meals. Also, to thank her for the books I began cleaning her apartment on a regular basis since she was too old for housework. Frequently I took her a plate of food from our evening meal.

We exchanged Christmas gifts but hers were wonderful items from her past. She gave Roy a leather case holding a syringe that had belonged to her grandfather, who practiced medicine in Kowaliga, AL between 1870-1890. She also gave us her father's hand painted Nippon tobacco jar, watercolor paintings from Japan, and a German bisque doll. These were our first antiques. Neither my family nor Roy's ever owned anything to pass down.

After being in Miss Slaton's first grade class, Roy excelled in elementary school and was double-promoted. At Woodlawn High school he was in the speech honor society, had roles in plays and an operetta and was elected student body president. He won the Jefferson County American Legion oratorical contest and lacked only one badge to become an Eagle Scout. But his favorite memory was playing catcher on the East Side All Star Baseball team's championship game at Rickwood Field.

Opposites did attract in our case. He could have been on a

billboard as an example of a successful high school student while my high school record and experiences epitomized the opposite. He was Mr Everything in High School and I was Miss Nothing. He loved it; I hated it. He was popular with everyone; I had almost no friends. Roy loved being in the spotlight; I didn't want to be noticed. He's got a mind like a trap; mine is more like a sieve. He's always lived by the golden rule while I spent most of my younger days getting even with others.

He was the emcee for the "Look Daddy" talent show for young people, televised on Channel 13 and did a commercial for Bama Peanut Butter. He enjoyed these activities so much he was unsure whether to go into radio and television or study medicine. Everett Holly, a local television executive and celebrity, told him to become a doctor.

Roy worked hard at the University of Alabama to achieve the good grades necessary to get into medical school. He did not allow himself weekend trips with his Pi Kappa Alpha fraternity brothers to places like New Orleans because he had to study.

He couldn't afford low grades. In one English class he sat in the middle of football players, and when he got a "c" on his first paper, he wondered if he was characterized as a student just interested in playing. So for his next paper he spent hours researching his "Physics of Flight" paper. He even found charts and photos in the National Geographic magazine to illustrate the points in his paper.

When the teacher gave out the graded compositions she said to him, "Who did this paper for you?"

He had all the notes and even the magazine he had used; but he was never sure she believed him and felt he was was the one cheated when he made only a "B" in the course.

Another time he didn't get the grade he felt he deserved. He and his roommate, Hobart Grooms, studied together for all the tests in their Russian History class. Roy consistently made a "B+" while Hobart, the son of a prominent judge, always made an "A" even though their answers were very similar.

At that time you could get into medical school after 100 college hours if your grades were good. So after two and a half years in college, Roy was accepted to the Medical College of Alabama at the age of 20. He received his B.S. degree after his first year in med school.

Margery Birdsong's daughter and her husband had to study to learn to a new language when they went as missionaries to a central Asian country (a closed country, so not named). They had four sons, ages one through six, Margery's grandsons, going with them.

"I knew they were answering the Lord's call but I was so sad at the prospects of not seeing them for a long, long time." Margery remembers.

"During the very week they were leaving that December, 1998, I received a Christmas card with a letter enclosed from the U.S. Postal Service stating that my mail had been tampered and they hoped I hadn't been inconvenienced," Margery said. "The card had been mailed to me four years earlier in December of 1994."

She said the belated Christmas card contained a poem which tells about the footprints of a man walking with the Lord in the snow. The man asked the Lord why there was just one set of footprints sometimes. The Lord said that was when he was carrying him ... during the most troublesome times in his life.

"I realized the Lord held up the delivery of that card for four years to encourage me with the poem, "Footprints" and to tell me He would be carrying me when I was troubled about my daughter and her family moving overseas. They were gone 15 years," Margery said, "and the Lord had me in his arms during most of that time."

The Lord also looked after Bill Moulton who as a Secret Service agent was assigned to find out who was stealing government checks.

The first man he talked to said he had taken the checks because someone had stolen his. The suspect was a huge, muscular man over six feet tall who had been arrested numerous times before, but not without a fight.

"You know, I'll have to take you in," Bill told him. "You will have to spend the night in jail, because the magistrate has probably left for the day. Do you have a weapon?"

The man handed over a large concealed knife.

When they arrived at the jail, the other officers were surprised Bill brought him in alone. In the past it had always taken several men to subdue him, at least two or three.

When Bill asked the man why he didn't resist arrest, like he had in the past, he said, "Because you treated me with respect."

Chapter 18

"A THERAPIST CALLED me today," Roy told me. "One of my patients, who is also seeing him, has been having the same nightmare over and over about our family. She told the therapist to call and tell us about her dreams.

He told us, "Several times she dreamed that Renee would be killed in a wreck when she was riding in a dark blue Buick Skylark. She wanted us to know so we wouldn't let Renee go out in a car of that kind."

Was this a warning - a message from God? Roy was certain he had never talked about our children or even named them to this patient.

We went to talk with our pastor.

"If this is a prophecy from God," Rev. Barker told us, "everything that was foretold will happen exactly as it had been revealed. If it is not from the Lord it won't be exact."

Rev. Barker told us there was nothing we could do to stop it but pray, which we were doing continually.

That week at a bridge party I was telling about the dream when a horn began to blow outside, in front of the house. The sound was coming from a new, dark blue Buick Skylark, the exact car mentioned in the dream. The owner of the car, Charles Jager, went out but could only stop his horn from blowing by disconnecting it. No one knew what caused it to start blowing.

In the Old Testament trumpets or horns were used to draw attention to extraordinary events, to warn Israel of danger or to call them for battle, while reminding them of God's protection.

The phone ringing late at night didn't normally disturb me. It was usually about Roy's patients, but this call at 12:20 a.m. jarred me awake. It wasn't about Renee but about Roy, our 19 year old son, who was not in when I went to sleep.

"It's bad, Jo Anne," Roy told me. "Little Roy has been in a wreck. He's in the emergency room at University Hospital. He may not live."

His BMW was dark blue.

Immediately, this Bible verse came to my mind, *"Do not be not anxious about anything but in everything, by prayer and petition, with thanksgiving, present your requests to God. And the peace of God, which transcends all understanding will guard your heart and your mind in Christ Jesus." (Philippians 4:6-7 NIV)*

At the hospital he was unconscious and we were told he probably wouldn't live. He had been thrown through the windshield of his car before he skidded across the asphalt and lawn on his face and head. His ear and eye had sustained injury.

But more threatening were indications of a serious closed head injury. On admission, his pupils were dilated and fixed and his arms and legs were stiffened into a rigid position, usually a sign of extensive brain damage.

As we waited Roy prayed, "Lord, you know our desire. Please let him live and let him recover. But we want your will regardless of the outcome. Just give us strength for what lies ahead. Help us, for we don't even know how to pray."

Roy was praying what Catherine Marshall called the Prayer of Relinquishment in her book, <u>Beyond Our Selves</u>. It is when someone prays for a good result in a dreaded situation, but still tells God they are ready to accept whatever He wills. On the Mount of Olives when he sweated blood, Jesus demonstrated this when he prayed, "My Father, if it is possible, may this cup be taken from me. Yet not as I will, but as you will." (Matthew 26:39 NIV)

As we waited we remembered and told each other promises, found in the Bible, thankful that we had been urged to memorize scripture. A real value of knowing God's word is in emergency situations when you can't or won't look in the Bible to find comfort or direction.

"Have I not commanded you? Be strong and courageous. Do not be terrified, do not be discouraged, for the Lord you God will be with you..." (Joshua 1:9-10 NIV)

Two young doctors, members of the Christian Medical Society came to pray and comfort us with more words from God.

"And we know that in all things God works for the good of those that love him, who have been called according to his purpose." (Romans 8:28 NIV)

With medicines, fluids and the ventilator helping him breathe, Roy's rigidity disappeared and his eyes began reacting to light. He was now headed to surgery to have a skin graft from his leg placed over the exposed, cracked skull, to repair his ear and to place a device deep in his brain to measure pressure and to allow blood and fluids to be removed from the brain, if needed. It would be several hours before he would be placed in intensive care so I went home to shower and see the accident scene.

"He will have no fear of bad news; his heart is steadfast, trusting in the Lord." (Psalm 112:7 NIV)

A freak April snow lay on the yards as I drove home, going by the accident scene on Chestnut Road. It occurred on a street I knew so well because it was part of our younger son's paper route which I drove daily. Roy's car had run off the road, grazing a mailbox, then re-entered the street, flipped and skidded on its roof over another mailbox across the street, before coming to rest at the far edge of that yard. The second mailbox belonged to an older lady whose mail and paper we delivered to her door each day. As I looked at the strewn wreckage and the blood on the snow, I could feel God's hand in this because of that particular spot for the accident.

Intensive care is a room of unconscious and unclothed people, held to earth by tubes and wires which graphically demonstrate our complete dependence on God and remind us how intense is His constant care of us.

134

"I have learned the secret of being content in any and every situation ... I can do everything through Him who give me strength." (Philippians 4:12-13 NIV)

Day after day our son lay there. The respirator breathed for him, the IV dripped in food, water and medicines, the EKG wires monitored his heart, the catheter drained his kidneys, and the shunt guarded against dangerously high pressure in his brain.

Little Roy's packed cell blood volume was dangerously low, so he needed Rh negative blood transfusions. Reverend Barker and another Briarwood minister, Tom Carrodine, both had his Rh negative blood, and donated their blood for him. I couldn't think of anyone's blood I would rather have pulsating through our son's body than theirs.

An infection caused his temperature to spike several times. His head swelled until it resembled a pumpkin. We had specific prayer requests for the countless people praying for him. I updated his condition almost daily on posters tied to our mail box at the street. Those prayers were answered as the swelling, infection and fever disappeared.

Roy's secretary, Reba Manfree, typed a Bible verse on an index card to encourage us. Each day she gave us a new verse.

Four nights after the accident I asked God that if our son was going to be all right, to let him open his eyes. In Intensive Care the next day, I questioned the chief neurosurgery resident about his condition.

"Nothing has really changed, but it's a good sign that he opened his eyes."

The tears began to pour as I said aloud, "Thank you, Father. Thank you." Then, I explained about my prayer.

"Don't get too encouraged," the resident said. "He's certainly not out of danger, and we won't know the long term effects for some time. The longer someone is unconscious, the grimmer the prospects."

But I knew from all those Bible verses not to despair. God was in charge.

For the next two days nothing significant happened.

We were taking an Old Testament class at Birmingham Theological

Seminary. Rev. Barker had just explained how David was able to face his giant problem, Goliath. He said everyone would face giant problems in their lives. David remembered what God had done for him in the past, and he acknowledged that it was God's fight, not his. Then David faced Goliath, doing all he could do physically, but trusting God for the results. I determined to do the same. Everything humanly possible was being done for our son. It was indeed up to God, so I would trust Him for the outcome. I knew He was trustworthy from His past dealing with me.

"Peace I leave with you; my peace I give to you ... Do not let your hearts be troubled and do not be afraid." (John 14:27 NIV)

Roy Jr. began to respond to commands by wiggling his toes, waving or opening his eyes. As he began to wake from his coma, he had to be restrained. Although unable to use his hands, he was able to jerk out the ventilator tube. He no longer needed it.

After 11 days in intensive care, he was moved to a room. His eyes would open but seemed unseeing. We didn't know if he was blind. And his attempts at speech were unintelligible.

Two days later when his father entered the hospital room before me, our son said, "Hi, Dad." We both burst into tears of thanksgiving. We knew he could see, he could recognize us, and he could speak.

Physical therapy began with Roy sitting in a chair, then standing, and finally taking those first halting, unbalanced steps, while being supported on both sides.

With slow, steady progress in speech and walk, Roy was transferred to Spain Rehabilitation. It was a sad place filled with teens and young adults who have forever altered their life with a moment of recklessness. Many were now permanently in wheel chairs and some could only communicate by pointing to letters on a board to spell out their message. We were not encouraged by the staff about our son. We were told he might never be able to live independently and might have to be institutionalized.

Roy Jr. was still confused as to the year, where he was, and his past history.

I reminded myself that Peter was able to walk on water as long as he kept his eyes on Jesus and did not look at the circumstances around him. I, too, learned that I wouldn't be despondent as long as I looked at what was possible with God and not at the medical forecast for our son. My husband knew too much and this knowledge kept interfering with his faith. He finally made himself forget what the world thought and remembered what the Bible taught.

Our son had to work on his balance and mental challenges as he recovered. He told me later his brain actually hurt when he tried to think. He hated the menial activities of stringing colored beads to match those already strung and practicing life skills at Spain Rehab, but he was slowly recovering. The staff, though, still gave us no hope of his complete recovery.

We celebrated his 20th birthday on the patio at Spain Rehab with a cake and ice cream for any of the other patients that were able to attend. Roy's friend, Roger Strick, brought two fellow band members and they provided music. Many of Roy's friends, including Roger's twin brother, Walter, and Shawn McCucheon, who had been so faithful in visiting him, attended the party.

Roy's girl friend, Matina Kanakis, continued to visit him frequently. She had talked to him while he was unconscious, encouraging him to wake up and letting him know she cared. I always felt he could hear her and that helped him wake up. I'll always love Matina. She helped him recover.

Roy Jr. was home on leave from the National Guard when the accident occurred. Because he wasn't a full-time student, he had been dropped from our health insurance. We didn't know we could get Cobra, which stands for Consolidated Omnibus Budget Reconciliation Act, insurance for him until the very last day of the grace period. This federal law allowed us to buy insurance with our previous carrier for up to 18 months coverage. We mailed in the check.

However, Blue Cross later said they never got the check and we had no coverage.

Not knowing what to do with our son when he was released, we decided to take a family trip to California with my Mother in her van. We left home with bills on the kitchen table totaling over $100,000 for Roy Jr.'s treatments.

In one of his rehab classes, I wrote down the title and author of the book the therapist was using and then ordered my own copy. We picked up where the professional had stopped and by the time we got home we had completed the book and he was a lot better.

Only one incident caused sorrow on the trip. Roy Jr. was still unsteady. One morning when we ate at McDonald's he spilled his breakfast on the floor. Randy made the mistake of laughing. Little Roy swung at Randy who ducked. Mother was right behind Randy and little Roy's fist hit my mother in the face. She had a black eye for over a week, and we all had anger and hurt feeling for even longer.

Back home the new bank statement included our cancelled check made out to Blue Cross for the insurance. God had saved us by making us aware of the fact that Roy Jr was uninsured and by providing the cancelled check, proving that we had gotten the supplementary policy on the last day it could be purchased. Not a coincidence.

As God had told me, Roy Jr. did recover. He was able to return to the University of Alabama, and by taking a light schedule, finish the class work for his degree.

But the greatest reward was the 180 degree turn in his attitude and actions. He now showed love to us and appreciation for what others did. And he no longer rejected God. What an answer to prayer! We'd asked God to change our son's mind. Although we would have never chosen this method, we were so thankful for his turn around.

Another blessing was his becoming reacquainted with his first girlfriend from the seventh grade, Hope Childers, who came to see him at Spain Rehabilitation. Matina told Hope she didn't need to come back to see our son, but Hope paid no attention. They began dating again after his release from the rehabilitation hospital.

Chapter 19

SPEAKING FROM EXPERIENCE, Pastor Don Glass said, "There is hope for addicts."

"I was a divorced, drug addict, living for myself, before I came to the Lord. One day I realized how bad off I was and broke down and said, 'If you are real come into my life.'"

God entered his life in 1988. That year Don was in a serious motorcycle wreck.

With the possibility of losing his leg he made a promise that if he got to keep his leg he would tell others that God is real and warn them of the danger of motorcycles. God answered that prayer.

"It was like a light come on and told me to start attending church where he rededicated his life. There he met the lady who four years later became his wife.

In May 1991 they were called by the Lord to start a church. In four and a half years he went from being a drug addict to pastoring a church.

When Randy got his driver's license, I lost my income from driving him on the paper route. Soon after he was chosen as one of Birmingham's two best newspaper deliverers in Birmingham and was honored at a dinner in New York City along with others who had won that award in their town, before they left on the winners' trip to

Switzerland. Later he quit delivering newspapers and began delivering pizzas. With such great tips Big Roy suggested I deliver pizza too.

"Would you have any patients then?" I said, not knowing if he was kidding or not. "What kind of a doctor has a wife who first delivered newspapers and then pizzas?" Instead, I did some freelance writing for the Baptist Hospitals. I also wrote a monthly column for the newly launched magazine, Just CrossStitch.

The franchise for the Birmingham News' Bluff Park delivery area was for sale. Because it was physically hard no other women were district managers. But it was a great opportunity so we got the huge loan to buy the business.

Six days a week I picked up the the newspapers from a conveyer belt at the Birmingham News office, loaded them into my van and took the newspapers to the carriers for the afternoon delivery. Then, I put papers in the vending machines. On occasion I would have to throw a paper route when a carrier was sick.

On Sundays at 4 a.m. Roy helped me do the same thing. This left us just enough time to dress before the 8 a.m. church service where we struggled to stay awake. We hated working those Sundays. But I especially hated the irate, ugly calls from customers who had not gotten a paper or didn't like where it was delivered. I thought *if that's all you've got to complain about you are very fortunate.*

I made good money during those years before I was told the Birmingham News would not renew my contract. I had to find a buyer for the franchise or I would lose my $100,000 investment. The man who sold to me had also had his contract cancelled. The Lord sent a buyer and I was able to repay the loan. The Birmingham News was later forced to pay $15.6 million to six former newspaper dealers who sued after the Birmingham News would not renew their contract. I wasn't one.

For a time I worked in a psychiatrist's office filing and typing up the doctor's notes on his patients' visits. I found I wasn't as crazy as some people. Some people may think that is debatable.

Renee considered several universities. But it had to be one that offered her a scholarship. She took the Presidential Scholarship at the University of Alabama where her brother was already a student.

That year we financed a 10 unit apartment complex on the campus, right across from Tutwiler Dorm. Then, both Renee and Roy had one bedroom apartments. First one and then the other was the apartment manager, renting out apartments and calling repairmen as needed. It was good training for them and freed us of most of the operation.

Renee joined Alpha Chi Omega sorority. With great grades she was tapped for eight honor societies including Mortar Board, and Phi Beta Kappa. She graduated magna cum laude in 1990 with a A.B. in English. After graduation, her friends moved in and ran the apartments for us for years. But eventually we no longer had contacts at the University.

I made frequent trips to Tuscaloosa to show the apartments, meet repairmen, clean and paint the units. I was glad to hire a student manager to free me from many of these duties even if I didn't know them personally.

Once when I opened the door to a 'vacant' apartment, a girl was inside. She said she had lived there for three months. Two other 'vacant' apartments were also occupied.

The student manager had rented the apartments with out telling us and kept the rent money. He had to find a new way to supplement his income after he was fired. That convinced us to sell the apartments. We had not listed it with a relator. At the apartments one day I came outside from cleaning and saw Roy had stopped cutting the grass and was talking to a man.

"Jo Anne," Roy said, "this man asked me who owned these apartments. When I told him we did, he said he would like to buy them."

"Hallelujah!" I yelled.

Later, Roy told me, "You shouldn't say 'hallelujah' when someone offers to buy something. Then, they'll offer you less."

But, we did sell the apartments for a good profit. I would have taken less.

Roy was pictured on billboards around Birmingham that said, "Choose a UAB doctor for Life." For 25 years he had been seeing patients at the Kirklin Clinic and teaching at the UAB Medical School. He continued to see patients but in 1991 retired from teaching and began to draw his retirement funds from UAB. As he was still employed by the Kirklin Clinic he didn't receive any retirement money from them.

The IRS said he owed taxes on all his retirement funds, not just those from teaching in the medical school and that he owed a large amount in taxes. We didn't have the money to pay that big tax bill.

Finally, Roy and our accountant convinced the IRS that he was only receiving retirement money from his years of teaching at UAB. Since he was still seeing patients at Kirklin, he wasn't receiving any retirement funds from them. We knew God was ultimately responsible for our missing another financial bullet.

One night when Roy got home told me, "I found you a job."

"I didn't know I was looking for one."

One of Roy's patient was scheduled for open heart surgery and needed someone to work in her gift shop in Forestdale, a community on the other side of Birmingham. I took the job. I had never been in sales, but I loved the interaction with customers coming to buy bridal or other gift items. I also enjoyed arranging displays.

The owner had a unique way of generating sales. She had her

customers register for items they liked. She kept this information on file along with their their birthdays, their wedding anniversary dates and their husband's office number. Then, before some gift buying date, she would call the husband and tell him about his wife's pre-selected items and their prices. The husband decided how much he would spend to get his wife something she really wanted. The gift would be wrapped and ready for him pick it up on his way home.

I continued working there when the owner returned after her recovery. In November she planned for the store to be open on Sundays for Christmas shopping. I couldn't work on Sundays so I quit.

Roy had other jobs in the 1990s. He became a proctor for the American Board of Internal Medicine, giving the board exams to doctors with different specialities once or twice a year. After a couple of years, the Board felt physicians shouldn't be giving the tests since they would be taking it themselves. I had helped administer the test, so I became the proctor, reading the directions aloud, timing the test, and watching to make sure there was no cheating. This job lasted five years until they switched to computerized tests.

Never one to turn down a lucrative job, Roy was also hired by several attorneys to testify as an expert witness for their medical cases.

During those days, the pharmaceutical companies marketed heavily to physicians - giving them tickets to concerts, plays, or sporting events. At dinner their current drug was discussed. Roy spoke for certain drug companies, introducing their new medicines to doctors.

On the way to and from work he listened to medical tapes to keep current on diseases and treatments. The Southern Medical Association offered these to physicians on the different specialities. Roy became the Endocrinology Editor for their "Dial Access" series. Then, he both made tapes on endocrine problems and got other physicians to record the latest information on their speciality.

While Randy and I attended graphic art classes at Bessemer Tech, Roy took a course in small engine repair at night. He was paired with the former crew chief for Bobby Allison, the race car driver. They got along so well that when the course ended, the former crew chief asked Roy to go into business with him repairing lawn mowers and other small engines. No one in the class knew Roy was a doctor.

Roy also took Richard Condrey's class at church on how to repair toilets.

When my brother, Robert, heard about Roy's new classes he called Roy's office at the Kirklin Clinic. "Let me speak to the toilet doctor," he said to the nurse answering the phone.

"What? This is the Kirklin Clinic," she said. "We don't have a toilet doctor."

"Yeah, you do. He works on toilets and repairs lawn mowers, too. I need some work done..."

"Is this a joke?"

"No. Just ask Dr. Roddam. He'll tell you about his outside jobs."

When Roy heard about the incident he knew who had called.

My brother, Robert, his wife, Jane, and their three sons, Nick, Jeff and Steve, lived near us. Robert had degrees and had worked corresponding jobs in chemistry, industrial engineering, pharmacy and law. He loved going to school. We kidded him that he wanted to retire right out of college. After practicing law for a while, he returned to pharmacy.

We have a gene in the family for practical jokes. It was well developed in Robert.

Once a mother came in to refill a prescription at the pharmacy department at the back of the store. She had her four-year-old daughter and her baby with her.

Robert told the little girl, "I sure like that baby. Would you give it to me?"

Putting her hands on her hips, the child said, "No. That's my baby."

Robert made an offer she couldn't refuse. "I'll give you a puppy for the baby."

She said, "O.K.," and told her mother, "Give him the baby. I want a puppy."

When her mother wouldn't swap, the little girl began to cry, getting louder and louder. They left with her still screaming for a puppy.

Another night, business at the drug store was slow. Robert was talking with a policeman friend when outside they saw an old man place a large trash bag in the garage container in front of the drug store. He then drove to the grocery store at the other end of the strip mall. They wondered what was in the garbage bag and why he had brought it and put in it the this garbage can, instead of at home. It was full of whiskey bottles.

The policeman took the bag and put on the hood of the man's car.

After stashing his groceries in his trunk, the old man got in his car before noticing the bag. They watched him drive back to the same garbage container and put the whiskey bottles back in it.

As he drove off, the policeman got his tag number, called in and got his address. When the store closed, Robert and the policeman took the garbage bag to the man's house and leaned it against his front door.

They didn't see his reaction when he opened his front door and found the bottles had followed him home. They wondered if he wasn't trying to keep his drinking a secret from his wife.

Robert raised Pomeranian dogs. Once when Robert was in the check out line at Walmart with lots of cans of dog food, the cashier, noticing all the dog food, said, "You must have a lot of dogs."

"Dogs? Dogs? I don't have any dogs."

"Then, why are you buying all that dog food?"

"Oh, the family is having a reunion, and I've been put in charge of making the meat loaf."

Chapter 20

THE SECOND LATE night call, that no parents wants to receive, came in at 2:30 a.m. Randy had been in a wreck with four of his friends and two of the boys were dead. They had just left a teenage party awash with alcohol and drugs. The parents were out of town.

Randy told us what happened. (Names have been changed.) "On leaving the party five of us loaded up in Steve Freeman's car when Mark Spencer got in the front, passenger seat. Mickey James told him to move because he had called shotgun. So Mark got in the back seat with Matt Young and me. I was in the middle.

"As we started barreling down Lime Rock Road I realized we would not be able to make the curve at the bottom of the hill. I started digging for my seat belt and said aloud, 'God, I want to live. I want to live.' I didn't get a chance to put it on. The car ran off the road at the curve directly in front of Vestavia Hills High School and hit the utility pole. None of us had on seat belts."

Matt Young was not injured. He sprinted to the nearby fire station. The paramedics were quickly on the scene. Both the driver and front seat passenger had died instantly. Taken to Brookwood Hospital, Randy's scalp and hair were sown back on with 66 stitches and both his broken arms were put in casts. Mark Stags who had minor injuries was seated in the back seat with Matt and Randy.

Randy, Mark and Matt, the three in the back seat, had survived but not without problems. They all felt guilty they had lived. Randy's constant questions for months were, "Why did I live? Why did my friends die?"

The Bible says there's a time to be born and a time to die. We do not have the mind of God to understand His timing for death, but we do know He is in charge of the universe and not a sparrow falls without his permission.

In many ways I felt responsible for Randy's risky behavior and his being involved in the wreck.

We were having problems with both our sons.

Sandy Wheeler, prompted by the Holy Spirit, wrote me a letter, telling me to never give up. The Bible verse she quoted was Gal. 6:9 NIV, "Let us not become weary in doing good, for at the proper time we will reap a harvest if we do not give up." I was thankful she cared enough to write that letter. True friends remind you that God is working.

Life wasn't pleasurable. My depression returned. I wanted to avoid other people. I didn't look at them. They might smile, and I didn't feel like smiling back. I would look down so they wouldn't see the hurt in my eyes. My teeth were clamped together like a vice. I didn't want to talk to anyone. When I did speak, there was no inflection in my voice. It sounded as dead as I felt. There was no hope, no answers, no ending. I might get small reprieves, but soon I was back in the rejection, the fear, the hate. What I hated most was myself. I wallowed in self pity while detesting my self-centeredness.

As I drove the car, frequently I heard a voice, not literally, but in my mind, that said, *"Drive in front of that truck"* or *"drive off that embankment and it'll all be over."* I thought about suicide weekly if not daily.

I was hanging on by my nails. Would I ever be free? I didn't have to watch soap operas. I was living one. I prayed. That's all I felt I could do to help either myself or my sons. It should have been the first thing I did, but you have to train yourself to seek God first before you try to solve problems. I knew the solution would always be from God's hand and not from my actions. But I kept forgetting that and trying to manipulate the situation as I had always done.

To avoid thinking about the problems, I escaped into reading novels or watching old movies on television - anything to keep my mind on something else - as I filled my days to pass the time. These have been called soft addictions, which rob us of so much time that at some point we wonder where our life has gone.

As I attempted to tune out my inner feelings, I tuned out other people too. My bridge playing friends did try to encourage me, but I felt so low. They could not relate to me. There was no one who understood. I doubted they wanted me for a friend. It seemed to me that I just waited. And I continued to play the old tape of "what if" I had done this or that.

But then I would remember the 'letter' that God sent me because He loved me and had died for me. I had kept that article about why God doesn't want you to commit suicide. I reread that article many times.

One thing for sure if I hadn't given up drinking, I would have become an alcoholic. Some time before, the Lord wanted me to stop drinking and He gave me an ulcer. At that time the cause of ulcers was thought to be from stress, lifestyle or improper diet, specifically spicy foods and alcohol. I had been drinking the previous two nights, so that could have been the cause of the episode or so I was told. I was hospitalized due to the pain. Not wanting to hurt like that again I quit drinking. Of course, I still had the stress. Years later scientists learned that ulcers are caused by a germ.

I had always like to drink, even as a child. Mama bought a bottle of wine every year to flavor her Christmas fruit cakes. She kept it in the china cabinet in the dining room. When I'd get home from school my brother was playing outside and my parents weren't home from work so I sampled the Mogen David grape wine. It was good. Lots of afternoons I'd have a little drink. When Mother needed the wine to flavor her fruit cake the bottle was empty. She though she knew who had consumed it. Poor Dad could never convince her it wasn't him. She never suspected her 10-year-old daughter.

If you see tears in my eyes just pray that I will put my focus back on Christ. For I know that He loves me. That was settled years ago. And nothing happens that He will not use for my good. So I just need to keep focused on God, then I too can persevere and not sink in the mire of unbelief or self pity.

My depression might have caused my distracted behavior - like washing Roy's cell phone in the pocket of his pants, pulling the towel into the shower before I turned off the water or trying to put on pierced earrings with the backs on the stems.

I did other crazy things too. I had a garage sale at my nephew's house. His whole neighborhood was having sales but there weren't any near his house. We didn't get many customers although I put out lots of signs. I found out why after the sale when my nephew retrieved the signs and told me I had put down the wrong address.

I wasn't the only one distracted. One day Roy told me about waiting to cross University Boulevard.

"It was the longest light. I waited and waited. I had just about decided to take my chances in the busy traffic when another person walked up and pushed a button on the light post. It turned the traffic light red and stopped the cars."

While Renee and Derek were away on vacation, they asked Roy to feed their dog and collect their mail. The dog food was kept in a big garbage can, outside the basement door. Another garbage can was beside it. Roy thought that was where he was to put their mail. Every day he put the mail in the second can. When Renee and Derek returned home there was no mail. Apparently, the garbage man looked in the can with dog food and recognized it was being used for storage so he didn't empty that one. But he emptied the other containing what he thought was trash.

My depression made me interpret "funny" comments made about me as disguised criticism. They had a ring of truth. If I can, I avoid people who tease like that.

While playing bridge, after I'd made a difficult contract, I was told, "I'd rather be lucky than smart."

I told my bridge group that they were my best friends, even though I didn't get to see them that often.

"Maybe that's why we are your best friends," one of them told me.

Once Roy said to me, "The mosquitos are eating me alive. Just walking from the house to the car several bit me."

"I wonder why they don't bother me."

"They only like sweet people."

Most of my help comes from reading God's word or from encouraging sermons at church. Frank Barker retired from the pulpit at Briarwood but the Lord sent another, terrific pastor-teacher, Harry Reeder.

Through Dr. Reeder the Lord taught me that we go to church to worship and not just to learn. I've always loved to learn, and I suppose I used knowledge to make me feel better about myself. But, that created the problem of making even church attendance about me. I tried to put the Lord on the throne of my life, but then I kept putting myself back on. Dr. Reeder spoke to me when he said it was not enough to know scripture. It was of little benefit if you didn't put it into practice.

Scott Spell knew how to put prayer into practice in the early 70s when his former church's bus broke down in the deserts of Colorado. He was with the youth choir when a hose burst on their church bus, letting out all of the coolant. The bus driver wrapped the broken hose with duct tape. But they still needed the coolant or water to refill the radiator.

This was before individual bottled water became popular. Cell phones, the internet and GPS were still in the future.

They knew where they were on that seemingly deserted highway. But with no way to call for help, the Minister of Music asked the youth to join with him as he prayed for rain. It was almost no time before they heard the sound of rain hitting the bus.

Now the need was to collect the water. The teens passed forward anything that could be used to catch the rain. Cookie tins, cups and plastic bags were used. As these items were filled, the water was poured into the radiator.

The rain stopped as the last drop was poured in. The driver announced there was enough water in the system to safely make it to a gas station for repairs.

"We were late for our planned destination on that day," Scott said, "but we knew our prayers had been answered immediately to meet our need. We, who witnessed it, will always remember. Great is thy faithfulness, O God my father."

Chapter 21

YOU MAY HAVE troubles but you never know what blessings are waiting just around the corner. Our first grandchild, Jane Anne Roddam, the daughter of Roy and Hope, arrived May 28, 1995.

It was nothing like having children - no responsibilities. How they turned out was now up to someone else. But I wanted to be a part of my grandchildren's lives. My grandmothers, each with a total of up to 30 grand-children, had too many to babysit any of them. My mother's mother actually said, "I raised mine. Now, you raise yours." Jane Anne was like the daughter I always thought I would have with my blue/green eyes and blond hair, but there the resemblance ended. For she came into the world with one goal - learning everything she could. And she would excel at it, beyond our proudest expectations.

All the good grandmother/grandfather names had been chosen. I refused to be Granny or Big Mama. I liked the idea of being called Beauty but Roy refused to be called Beast. I don't know why because we finally decided we'd be Honey and Bear, another animal name for him.

Before we could get used to being grandparents, Roy and Hope announced they were expecting again. Hope's mother warned her that this had to be the last; she refused to baby-sit more than two children.

But man proposes, and God disposes. The ultrasound showed two babies were coming. There are no twins in our family. Hope has twin sisters but Hope was the one to deliver twins - 17 months after their first child. Julia Guice Roddam, and John Franklin Roddam arrived December 6, 1996. All of us took turns caring for three babies under the age of two. How different from when I had three little ones with no help.

Julia was like the daughter I did have with the black hair and brown eyes from the Roddam genes. She could have passed for Renee's daughter. Our first grandson, John, was just a delight, and we couldn't tell who he looked like.

When the twins could climb out of their cribs, they pulled over a small lingerie chest. John wasn't injured but Julia had to have stitches on her eyelid. Some children have died when the furniture they were climbing on fell on them. For protection Hope and Roy put them in "cages", mesh tents zippered on the outside of the cribs. They looked pitiful, but I wished I had those cages when mine were little.

Soon John learned how to escape and was found asleep zipped in Julia's bed. When he started releasing Julia, Hope put safety pins on the zippers to hold them in place. That kept them corralled for about six months until John ripped the plastic straps that held the mattress, allowing him to escape underneath the bed. Then, only spanking kept them in their cribs at night.

Unlike the twins, Jane Anne never got out of her bed. That was against the rules. She acted like the perfect child, but whenever Hope wasn't looking, she pinched the twins. She was like me after all.

John spent his toddler years trying to escape not only from his crib, but also from the confines of clothes. He was found nude frequently only wearing his shoes, which he couldn't remove because they were doubled knotted.

Julia not only looked like her father, she also had his gene for accidents. Starting with the stitches in her eyelid at age one, she was again sewn up after she opened her leg to the bone when she fell down the front steps. She had stitches for a cut knee and broken arm twice. Her worse mishap was when a quarter got caught in her trachea which had to be surgically removed. Thankfully, the Lord prevented the quarter from blocking her air and suffocating her.

Her father, Roy Jr., visited emergency room for nine stitches when he fell in a shoe store. Later, when the playground swing hit him, he required four stitches, and at little league tryouts, both his permanent front teeth were chopped off when he was hit by a bat.

Mother was keeping the children while we were at a football game when Little Roy had his worst accident. He and his bike rolled backward down a concrete embankment at Mt. Brook Junior High School, two blocks from Mother's house. Little Roy, eight, crawled out of the ditch bleeding from multiple cuts and scrapes, from bitting through his lip and from an injured hand. He and Renee began walking back to Mother's house.

A man and his wife in a passing car, saw he was injured and drove them to Mother's. Little Roy needed medical attention but Mother felt she couldn't take him and leave my elderly grandmother home alone with a broken arm. It seems unreal but Mother allowed that unknown couple to take our son to Montclair Baptist emergency room. But strangers were trusted more in that kinder, gentler time and they truly were Good Samaritans. My thoughts about Mother's actions were not nearly as kind.

How could the hospital treat a small boy without some relative being there to authorize it and pay for it? I don't know ... but the hospital did clean him up, put stitches in his cheek and lip and put a cast on his broken hand.

Before picking up the children at Mother's after the game, we went by our house where we found a bloody child's hospital gown on our sofa. Mother, my grandmother and the children had gone by our house to get Little Roy a shirt since the hospital had cut off the one he was wearing. Frantic, we called to see what had happened before we picked them up.

When Kathy McGinnis was five years old she fell out backwards from a two story window onto the concrete sidewalk below. She didn't hit her head and was miraculously unhurt. Her parents tried to keep her in bed but she begged to go swimming until they finally let her go. The doctor had not found anything wrong with her except a small scrape on one arm. How does she explain it?

"All I can figure is an angel caught me," she says.

Our next grandchild was Renee's and Derek's first child, Robert Reid Richesin, who arrived November 30, 1998. Renee and I painted all his nursery walls with scenes from the life of Peter Rabbit.

Since Renee was working as a psychiatrist, I kept Reid and drove him to her office to nurse. It was pure pleasure keeping and spoiling him. He was happy too, until baby number two arrived.

Ross Roddam Richesin arrived August 4, 2000.

"If you want him, you can have him," Reid tried to give him away to anyone who came to see him.

But Ross loved his big brother and as they grew they enjoyed each others' company as long as there were no grown-ups around. Reid didn't want to share all the spoiling he got from the adults in his life.

Some people believe man is basically good but the Bible says we are all sinners. I found that to be true. I know I was basically bad. From the crib upward babies want their own way. They act as if the world resolves around them and make trouble when thwarted. Children have to be taught to share and think of the other person. Some adults, like me, are still trying to master that consistently. But at last my depression was gone. Who can be depressed with grandchildren?

Renee's boys helped plant and cultivate flowers and vegetables. They never knew most of the world looked on that as work.

They sure didn't take after their grandfather. As a child Big Roy and his cousin, Wallace Franklin, would spend time each summer at their maternal grandparent's farm near Leeds. AL . They experienced life there as the older generation had with no running water, no electricity, no indoor plumbing and no transportation except a mule and wagon. On Saturdays, Papa Franklin allowed the boys to ride in the back of the wagon, letting tin cans, held with string, clatter along on the ground, as they rode to Birmingham for supplies.

Once when Papa Franklin told them to plant some peas. They were in a hurry so they just dug a hole and put all the peas in it. They learned that crime doesn't pay when all the peas came up in a thick mass. Their grandfather was angry with them.

Reid and Ross loved to gather vegetables. But they weren't allowed to pick the okra, because it makes your hands sting. What you can't have you always want, and Reid was determined to have the joy of cutting the okra. When Ross was offered a reward of anything because of his good actions, Reid didn't urge him to ask for a trip to Disney World or some expensive gift, he told him, "If I were you, I'd ask to pick the okra."

Reid finally convinced us that he was up to the task when he put on a long sleeve shirt and gloves. He had scissors to cut the okra off the plant. Then he learned it's just not that great.

Ross had his own way of thinking. At the beginning of the fourth grade his grandfather asked him what courses he would be taking that year.

"All of them," he said.

As with most siblings they see things differently. Reid wouldn't be caught dead at a garage sale while Ross, as a young child, loved to purchase great toys and sports equipment at them. Asked what car they would like one day, Reid named some sports car, Ross said he'd get a used Honda that got good gas milage.

At that time Ross was like us; we've never been into cars. When we married we had three cars. Roy had a Chevy and I had the newly won Pontiac and the Buick Skylark which I'd just finished paying for.

Eight years later I had three toddlers ridding in a VW bug. We wondered why Roy's parents bought a brand new Ford station wagon until they insisted on swapping it for our beetle. They were worried about the safety of their grandchildren.

Roy bought one of the first imported Isuzu and drove it for years. He loved that car. It's diesel engine got 50 miles per gallon in town. There weren't many diesel cars so gas for it was cheap. But it wasn't very pretty, especially on the inside. Leaving the children with the grandparents Roy and I once headed to Florida to do some touch up painting. Roy put an almost full gallon of paint on the back seat. The lid wasn't on securely and when he slammed on the brakes, the paint fell over pouring the paint out in the car.

One Sunday Rev. Barker stressed that Christians should not live ostentatiously such as driving expensive cars to impress others. I came on home with the children but Roy didn't come right away. When it became later and later, the children became concerned.

"He may be driving around Briarwood's parking lots, not to impress others with the kind of car he drives but to impress them with his humility as shown by his car." I was teasing. Roy never felt a need to impress anyone, as I did. I was yet to learn that the only one you live for is the Lord.

Several years later Roy drove the Isuzu through some deep water. From then on it developed a loud squeak. Not a soft little sound, but a noise that could be heard more than a block away. You could hear us coming, and people would turn to see what was making that noise. It got so bad that when he drove to the country club, even his golf buddies told him he needed to get another car. He finally agreed. I went shopping, comparing prices trying to find the best deal on a new car. While I was out of town he called to tell me he'd bought a car.

"What did you get?"

"Another Isuzu."

He bought a used one just two years younger than the one we had sold - it was still eight years old.

The next car we bought was a used, 1994 red Honda which I drove for a while. When our oldest son needed a car we gave it to him. In a couple of years he listed it for sale. We bought it and gave to our younger son. When he was ready to sell it Big Roy needed a car, so we bought it again. Honda makes great cars, this one especially. After all, we purchased it three times.

Once when we had an old car repaired, Roy returned the next day to get work done on the ten-year-old truck he had inherited from his father. The next week another older car of ours needed brakes so Roy took it to the same repair shop.

"How many of these old clunkers do you have?" the owner asked Roy.

I was waiting for a break in the traffic to turn right when I was hit in the rear by the car behind me. I told the other driver how sorry I was and he said not to worry, "It wasn't your fault."

"You wonder why these things happen," I said.

"Well, we know it is for a reason," said the man who turned out to be a Christian.

Although there was little damage, we swapped insurance information. Later, the other driver called to tell me that we had no insurance. Apparently, we threw away the insurance company's notice with some junk mail and now our car insurance had lapsed. We renewed it that day.

The next week Roy was driving us to Mobile on Interstate 65 South. He looked in the side window and seeing no car he pulled out into the left lane. A car, trying to pass us, was in the blind spot and it hit our car. The collision knocked the other car back across our side of the freeway, where it rolled several times before it reached the bottom of the ditch, adjoining the right lane.

Roy parked on the shoulder and went down to see about the other driver. She was wearing her seat belt, which prevented her being thrown from the car. The woman got out of her car and said she wasn't injured. Roy told her she should be checked out at a hospital, but she said she was fine. About three weeks later we learned she was suing us for $50,000 in damages in addition to the $200,000 our insurance company paid her. We learned she had a witness who would testify that Roy did not talk to her at the accident scene. She even claimed that Roy had not called to check on her condition.

But Roy had gotten her card at the accident scene. He had also called her twice on his cell phone and the cell phone company had a record to prove it. The judge threw out her suit for the additional amount.

But it was God that had saved us. The woman wasn't injured. And the previous rear end bump let us know we needed to renew our car insurance. God is always working behind the scenes.

Chapter 22

IN 1998 MOTHER said it was time to move in with us. Roy agreed.

She had recently lost all her savings, over $50,000 to a confidence man. She trusted him because he was her insurance man and a church choir director. I questioned and warned her because it sounded too good to be true. She got huffy and told me it was her money.

"You are right. If you want to give him all your money, do so. It is your money."

So, she lost all her savings - enough to have had a comfortable old age. He tried to get her to finance her house in order to have more money to 'invest', but she didn't. He was arrested, tried and sent to prison, but she would never get back her savings. Several other people were also bilked.

She had always looked after her family members, helping them, even financially, on a limited basis. She was a confident, in-charge type of person. Now, she was beaten and defeated. Mother sold her house and moved into Renee's old bedroom.

She could take care of herself physically and go wherever she wanted. She and her sister Myrt grew a big garden iat Myrt's house in Boaz, Al. Mother was in her 80s and Myrt was almost 90 but you wouldn't know it. They grew enough vegetables for several families, having learned how to garden as children.

They taught their children to work for the extras they wanted - such as a car. When you work and save for any item you appreciate it more than things you get without effort.

After Myrt died, we built two raised beds in our backyard for Mama to continue growing vegetables. She never wanted to waste space on flowers. As she aged, I assumed more of the physical work. For her, spring meant time to plant. And if I didn't have the ground ready, she would motivate me by saying, "I guess I can do it." I learned my gardening and manipulating skills from her.

Mother lived to age 95 with heart failure and an abdominal aneurysm. She died Dec. 30, 2008. Both Roy's parents died from strokes. Roy's father, 84, died Feb. 12, 1996 and his mother, 89, died Nov. 5, 2005. Diseases run in families and you inherit their genes so it is good to know what killed your ancestors because you may be prone to the same illnesses.

After forty years of practicing medicine, mainly at UAB, Roy retired completely in 2003. He had moved from student to instructor and finally to full professor in 1978.

I thought that having him home would create more work for me. But I didn't need to be concerned. He eats raisin bran cereal every morning. When we first married I cooked him bacon and eggs for breakfast. After a while he told me to stop because it was making him fat. Each day for lunch he eats chicken noodle soup. And like his breakfast, he prepares it himself.

If I could just find something he would like to have every night for dinner ...

I didn't have to worry about him being underfoot too much either. Working to perfect his hobbies of golf and bridge kept him out of the house.

Over the years he'd studied and practiced the grip, the stance and the swing for golf, resulting in many tournament wins in his flight. Most of our silver-plated serving pieces are those from his tournament wins. And in the Southern Senior games he frequently played free on the money he had won the previous week. His best ever score was 66 when he won the Christian Golfers Association's tournament at Waynesville, N.C. in 2005. In 2017 he hit a hole-in-one at the Southern Senior Tournament. That was his third hole-in-one.

One of his golf buddies told him, "Roddam, you are so boring. All your balls go straight down the middle. You miss seeing so much - all the flora and fauna we see off on the right and left of the fairway. And when you putt you have just a short time to enjoy the greens."

He expressed how lucky Roy was.

" Yeah," Roy replied, "like Gary Player said, 'The more I practice the luckier I get.'"

Roy was playing golf two days a week with different groups and frequently practicing on other days. One of his golf buddies had to give up the game. He said every time he played, he got teed off. Of course, he said he wasn't very good but reminded them, the proof is in the putting.

For years we exercising mentally by playing party bridge with my old friends from college. One of those friends, Ann Relfe, told us one night about losing the diamond from her engagement ring. Kneeling by her bed she prayed about the loss and then looking down she saw the diamond on the carpet.

The next week while working in the kitchen I heard a faint sound. Wondering what it was I looked down and saw that my diamond was missing. I got down on my hands and knees and searched until I found it. God had warned me before it happened.

Years later Roy and I were moving dirt and I stopped to go buy grass. When I got back I noticed my engagement ring was missing. I returned to the garden shop but didn't find my ring.

I prayed on the way back, "Lord, I know it's just a thing but I've had it a long time and I'd like to keep it. But if I can't find it; it is all right."

"It wasn't at the shop. It could be anywhere. I guess it's gone," I said putting on my work gloves. Then, I felt it. The ring was in the glove.

Eventually, most of these bridge games stopped due to death, divorce or couples moving away. Today's young adults don't take the time to learn this stimulating game. Lessons are available at the Birmingham Duplicate Bridge Club

I lamented to Sandy Wheeler and Barbara Curtis, two members of the Ladies Bridge Club, that Roy never had much opportunity to play bridge now that he had the time. So the three of us decided to form a duplicate bridge club with Roy as the only male member.

In duplicate bridge the same pair or partners play the same hands as all others sitting in that direction, either north/south or east/west to see who can make the most tricks or cause the opponents to score less than the others playing those hands.

Roy discovered Birmingham Duplicate Bridge Club, and we began paying to play there one or two times a week. Roy also began playing bridge with three other men on Thursdays at Trinity Methodist Church.

One of the Trinity players asked Roy to join his civic organization. We were invited to meet the members at a dinner at the Harbert Center, a high rise building in downtown Birmingham often used for parties and conventions. When we arrived we followed groups of people up to the glass-enclosed top floor. The lavish cocktail dinner spread was as spectacular as the view overlooking the city. We enjoyed steak, shrimp and lobster with the usual hors d'oeuvres of cheeses, dips, chips and vegetables. The dessert selection was awesome. We walked around enjoying the nicest cocktail party we'd ever attended.

But, we didn't see a person we knew, not even the man who invited us. We made small talk with several people. Then one of the strangers remarked that the hosts, a large, prominent law firm, always had great food. No wonder we didn't know anyone; we were at the wrong party.

We found the civic group downstairs, seated and eating the usual chicken dinner. We couldn't eat a bite.

Three years after retiring, Roy was named an Alabama Laureate for the year 2006. Fellow physicians give two awards yearly to doctors who are members of the American College of Physicians. Also shortly before his retirement Roy was named one of the Best Physicians in America. But the honor he liked best was when his grandson, John, chose him as his hero and wrote about it in the elementary school book that they produced.

John didn't know that Roy was a real hero. We were trying to leave early to start driving home after a week's vacation in Colorado but so many things went wrong that we were held up for over an hour before leaving Vail.

We were almost to Denver, headed up a long, steep mountain on Interstate 40 when we passed a group of people staring at a man lying on the shoulder of the road. He wasn't moving, and no one was doing anything to assist him. The people didn't seem to know what to do.

Roy stopped the car. The bicyclist had fallen on his descent down the hill. His blue color confirmed that he wasn't breathing. Fearing he might have a broken neck, Roy carefully opened his mouth and saw that his tongue was obstructing his breathing. Still being careful of his neck, Roy was able to pull the man's tongue forward allowing him to breathe. He was beginning to improve when the ambulance arrived and took him on to a Denver hospital. Without Roy opening the airway, he would have died before they arrived.

Roy called later and found out the patient had a blood clot in his brain but still had a good prognosis.

If we had left on time, instead of being hindered, Roy would not have been there to save that man's life. So, now when I am delayed, I realize it may be for some reason known only by God.

Another time while in the Air Force Roy received a Sikorsky Winged-S Rescue Award for those using a Sikorsky helicopter for a life saving rescue. Roy was flown out to care for and bring back to the hospital a Japanese fisherman who had lost his hand in a fishing mishap.

Over the years Roy saved the lives of at least four people in situations, other than in his regular care of his patients.

All the grandchildren have taken after their grandfather in enjoying golf. As soon as they could hold a golf club he had them hitting balls. The twins both made the golf teams at Vestavia High School. Earlier, Julia played soccer. John excelled at baseball, earning a trip to Cooperstown NY but John's real love is fishing.

Reid played soccer and competed successfully in bicycle racing as he was maturing. In 2014 he began competing and winning money in nationally recognized races. The next year he was asked to join the Hincapie Junior development team which provided him a road bike, a time trial bike and accompanying clothes and gear.

Reid is now studying international business at the International School in Paris, France.

Ross played all the little league sports well - football, baseball and basketball.

We had a wonderful trip to upper state New York to watch Ross play baseball at Cooperstown, the birthplace of the sport. The last game they played there was against a team from Mt Brook, AL. They played at the famed Elmer Doubleday Baseball Field. The other team did not have enough players so Ross played right field for them, when he wasn't batting or on base. Ross's team was behind one run with the bases loaded with two outs when one of Ross's team mates hit a fly to right field. Ross, showing true character, had to catch the fly which prevented his team from tying and then possibly wining the game.

This was not Ross's first example of integrity. Once a younger boy who was visiting had never seen miniature airplanes and had a wonderful time playing with Ross's. When his family was ready to leave Ross gave him a sack of the little airplanes. No one had suggested that to Ross.

In middle school he began to run track. As an 8th grader Ross won his age group in the Mercedes half marathon race in 2015, setting a new record of one hour and 25 minutes. He did well in mountain bike, winning 2nd overall in the state for high school freshmen boys in 2016. He graduated from Vestavia High School this year, 2019, and attends Birmingham Southern College.

We encouraged the grandchildren to do well academically by paying for good report cards. And we gave them small amounts of cash for other things. Maybe we overdid it because Julia told us, "It would be much easier for us if you just installed an ATM machine."

Julia would really benefit from that now. She is living in New York City working as a jewelry designer intern and will continue working for them after her internship.

John is a senior at Auburn and Jane Anne has completed her course work in medical school. She is interested in pediatric surgery.

In 2008 we took all the family to Washington D.C., New York City and Philadelphia, Pa. Because gasoline was almost $4 a gallon and we'd need three or four cars for 12 people, Hope suggested we ride the train. The three cities we visited have subways so there was no need for cars. Plus, we didn't have to find parking places.

Jane Anne wanted to be seen on television on her 13th birthday when the Today Show broadcasts people waiting outside their studio. Ten of us left for the 15 day excursion. Roy Jr. stayed home to work. Renee's husband, Derek, joined us in Washington and Roy Sr. in New York City.

We loved the train. We could sit together, play games at tables, buy food or eat what you had brought and walk throughout the train. Rocking side to side made walking an adventure for me. I was afraid I would end up in someone's lap.

We got off the train in Washington to spend a couple of days touring our nation's capital. All the government buildings and the Smithsonian were free. We only paid to see the Spy Museum and take a bus tour of the city. There was so much to see with all the memorials, monuments and other buildings.

Because it was Memorial Day weekend we saw a wonderful parade and many costumed actors demonstrating colonial life at George Washington's home, in nearby Mt Vernon, VA.

We boarded the train for New York City and a couple of days visiting all the tourist sites there. Then did the same thing in Philadelphia and in the Amish area nearby.

We saw so many museums, buildings, homes and historical sites that our grandson, John, remarked, "This is like having social studies everyday." It's not his favorite subject. The rest of us loved it.

Chapter 23

IN THE LADIES bridge club, we all faced hot flashes and brown spots together. We celebrated that we didn't have to shave under our arms since hair no longer grew there. But, actually, the hair just moved up to our chins. I thought we were getting nicer as we aged; we no longer pointed out each others' faults. But as facial hair increased, our ability to see it decreased. It wasn't tact, which is pretending you don't notice, that kept us from speaking, we just couldn't see it. Our new favorite beauty product was hair remover. To improve their vision most of the ladies then got contact lens, because their glasses were fogging up from hot flashes. Soon it was time for cataract surgery.

By far the worst complaint of growing old, of all things, accompanies a sudden, hardy laugh. It frequently causes you to wet your pants. At the same time our sense of smell is also decreasing. That is a bad combination.

My bridge buddies were always full of advice. We don't have to pay to see counselors because we have each other. I found, though, that It's better to be vague if your answer wouldn't be kind. Purr more, scratch less.

The bridge club was responsible for my going into business. One year for our annual, dirty Santa game, I made a Santa Claus face purse which they kept taking away from each other. Another year I made another one with a different face design. Again, my bridge friends fought over it. I thought if I could get the purses produced in China,

I might be able to make some money. The few I could sew by hand would only allow my idea to be stolen.

Not long after that, I met a young Chinese lady at church. During our conversation she asked if I attended the Thursday morning Bible study.

"No, I don't. But why do you ask?"

"Oh, I was hoping you'd go with me."

"I will."

That started a friendship. From then on Sharon Tang was like an adopted daughter. She, her husband and young son celebrated all the holidays at our home.

After about a year I asked her, "Sharon, do you know anyone in China who could make some purses for me?"

"My husband has a friend who has a purse factory."

What an answer to an unspoken prayer. I made nine prototypes in different sizes and materials and sent them off to China. Then, the factory replicated them and mailed back the samples. I took these to the Atlanta Merchandise Mart to show them to buyers who placed orders. I ordered a minimum amount of each style. Many customers were eagerly awaiting their purses so when they arrived I sent them right out. Never having had a business, I did not know to check for quality. Later, I discovered that some were sloppily made. I corrected those I could. The home office of the manufacturer was in Hong Kong and that is where the samples were made, but the factory was out in a Chinese providence, where there was no quality control.

The purses, I was showing and offering for sale, were the samples which were perfectly made. As a Christian, I knew it was only right to ship the perfectly made purses to my customers. I had boxes left from which I could chose correctly made ones to ship, but I felt like I couldn't order more. So, for a couple of years I sold the 'good' ones to hospital gift shops, who were my best customers, and at shops I visited on selling trips. Eventually, I was selling less than the cost of all the business licenses. I learned a lot, and I'll always be glad I tried. But, the Lord closed that door which He had opened.

Old age comes sooner than you think, as you become more forgetful. But really sometimes much of life is better forgotten.

I didn't feel old until I had a fall at age 72. I slipped and fell, hitting my shoulder and face on the concrete sidewalk as I was taking diapers for my Chinese daughter's new baby girl. The terrible pain told me something was broken. Roy eventually got the voice mail and arranged for an orthopedist to see me at St. Vincent's Hospital. His office x-ray showed three breaks in the bone near the ball of my left shoulder. He sent me to the hospital for a scan.

"If there is another break," Dr Johnson told me, "I will have to do a full shoulder replacement."

God answered my prayer. There were no other breaks. I was given medication for pain relief until I returned the next day for surgery.

Though many things about my hospital stay are thankfully foggy, God put this thought into my mind: "Is there someone here who needs to hear the Good News?"

On the way to surgery I asked the two people pushing my gurney the two evangelism questions. Their answers revealed that they were trying to get to heaven by doing good works instead of putting their faith in Christ's work on the cross on their behalf. Based on their works answers, I gave a short, gospel presentation. The Holy Spirit opened their eyes and they prayed to receive Christ. I was placed in a "holding area" for some time before actually being taken into the operating room. The nurse who was with me also prayed to receive Christ. I don't remember those three peoples' names.

When Hope, my daughter-in-law arrived, she began filling out the Spiritual Birth Certificates found in the Evangelism Explosion booklets, "Partners in Growing" for those who prayed - Donna, Robin, Carrie, Evelyn and one more. Also a male nurse received the assurance of his salvation. On leaving the hospital, Roy led a young father pushing me in a wheelchair in a prayer to accept Christ as Savior and Lord. That made the pain so much more bearable.

This experience reinforced my belief that the Lord is waiting for us to open our mouths and be used by him on the battle lines.

On my first visit to Over the Mountain Rehab, one of the physical therapists prayed. Later, another person there for treatment also committed their life to Christ as did a cleaning lady at the building.

That's twelve people, almost a person for each of the 13 screws put in my shoulder.

Growing old doesn't mean you've automatically arrived spiritually. Maybe your sins are not as overt or as frequent, but I continued having to confess some over and over.

"Don't even mention that man's name," I told my husband as were driving to church one Sunday morning. "In fact, I don't ever want to hear his name again ... for the rest of my life."

"He didn't do anything to you," Roy said. "You must not hold grudges ..."

"Stop. If you don't hush we are going to have a fight," I interrupted him. "Don't let him cause us to argue."

Of course, God wasn't through talking with me about my attitude.

In Sunday School that day Michael Mulvaney said he would be teaching on the main topics from Proverbs. "The third or fourth most mentioned topic is anger," he said. "Often anger is caused by not forgiving others."

I noticed Roy had a slight smile on his face.

"Forgiveness is a completely unnatural act that goes against our sin nature," Mulvaney said. "We can say we forgive but we still want to hear that we were right or we want to be praised for being so forgiving."

I saw Roy looking at me out of the corner of his eye.

"Jesus taught in the parable in Matthew 18 that when someone offends you, you must forgive them," Mulvaney continued. "A rich ruler forgave his servant a huge debt which the servant could never repay. Then the servant refused to forgive a paltry debt owed him by a fellow servant, and had him thrown in jail. When the ruler found out he had the first servant thrown into jail, too.

"Like the unforgiving servant, we owe a debt to God so great we could never repay it. So we certainly should be willing to forgive the small wrongs or affronts done to us."

Mulvaney suggested we consider each act of forgiveness as an offering or gift to the Lord to thank him for paying for our sins. He said that Israel used stones to build monuments to remind themselves and their children of the miracles God had done for them. Each time we forgive someone, he told us to visualize a stone with that person's initials on it, being presented to God. It was to remind us that we are doing this in appreciation for what God has done for us.

I thought of so many people that I had not truly forgiven. I realize that their offenses were infinitesimal in comparison with my forgiven sins.

I confessed my lack of forgiveness. With the God's help I would forgive that man. Forgiveness includes not telling anyone about the offense and even when you think about it, not dwelling on it.

God continues to use Roy to teach me and change me, even if at the time I resent it. My Christian life has been one of sl-o-o-o-w growth. Roy is a quick change artist. When he realizes his sin, he confesses and moves on. For him Christian principles are easily understood and applied.

I write down as much as I can of the sermons and the Sunday School lessons. I feel like the more senses I can engage in taking in the message the better I will remember it. But while I take copious notes Roy just listens. On the way home he asks me what were the most important points.

My brain is blank. I struggle to remember any of the points I wrote down. "Can I get back to you after I read over my notes?" He ends up telling me what I should have remembered. The next Sunday we repeat the same actions.

Roy was the first one to teach me not to make derogatory remarks about others. Then, the ladies bridge club reenforced this by example.

Over time Roy helped me see that even if I had made my Daddy an idol, I could be cleansed of that sin by confession. Sometimes God has to remove everything we rely on so that we will have to turn to Him. That's what He had to do in my case.

If I wanted to change my marriage I needed to change myself. My bad attitudes led me to bad feelings and even bad actions. I should have revealed more about myself and asked more questions. Too many people forget that even if your feelings change, your commitment made to your mate never does. We knew we were in it for life. But I agree with Billy Graham's wife, Ruth, who said, "Divorce was never an option. But murder was considered."

I expected Roy to meet all my needs, but only God can do that. I was to be a helpmate for my husband, but I frequently was not. Instead of being submissive, I was combative. Advice is free, counseling is not. I didn't look on Roy as a counselor so I told him, "If I want your advice I'll ask for it."

However, I always give him plenty of advice.

"You tell me how to drive, how to dress, how to eat..." Roy said

"You should appreciate my help."

"You are the one that needs help. Help is not controlling. You are always correcting me. You've been correcting me the 43 years we have been married."

"But if you get things wrong, I have to tell you. I'll try to do better. Oh, but it's 45 years we've been married."

When I first began delivering flowers to members in nursing homes I forgot to go one Monday. Renee had asked me to sit at her house that day because workmen were going to be inside replacing some windows and she had to be at work. I'm not sure that God didn't have me forget to go to church that day because both of the men prayed to receive Christ. That day was the only time they would be at Renee's.

I have forgotten to show up for parties, bridge games, even dinners. It was forgetting dental appointments - repeatedly - that was the worst. I have to face the dentist all the time. He's my son-in-law. His office is threatening to start double booking when I have an appointment.

I now put stick-up notes on the computer or exit door as reminders.

I had my ears pierced so I would stop losing earrings, but I lost some of those too. I hid my treasured jewelry to prevent it from being stolen if we had a break-in. They are safe now - even from me. I can't remember where I put them. I'll often find things I had hidden and didn't even know they were missing. Recently I signed up to attend a breakfast conference at church on "Brain Health" to help my memory, but I forgot to go.

I found that apologizing mentally to someone would relieve my conscience so much that I'd forget to tell them. But what are mental apologies or other good intentions if you don't follow through? It's not a virtue if you don't do it. I found I held others accountable for their actions while I forgave myself based on my intentions.

Seniors are notorious for forgetting. I saw that when I was young and had a garage sale for an older couple who couldn't have one at their house. While waiting for the sale to start I got out a deck of their cards to play solitaire and found $100 hidden in the deck.

But I am like the hymn writer of Amazing Grace, John Newton, who said "My memory is fading and my mind is gone. But I know two things: I am a great sinner and Christ is a great savior."

We all go though life thinking nice things about others but we may keep those thoughts to ourselves, when it would be so easy to affirm that person by giving them the compliment.

Each morning I try to remind myself to be nice to others - to build them up.

Parents want their children to be good like they remember themselves being. But each year we remember less and less about our bad actions, words and thoughts. Having less to keep quiet about is a blessing. One of the wonderful things about aging is that you forget so many embarrassing events.

No telling what Roy has done that I've forgotten.

But I learned you can't trust some old sayings. You've heard that an apple a day keeps the doctor away. Don't believe it. I put an apple on Roy's pillow for years. It never did any good.

Chapter 24

AGING CAUSES MANY body parts to wrinkle, sag or ache when you move. A friend at church, Banks Farris, told me, "If it don't hurt, it don't work. The only way you know it is working is that it is hurting. "

When Roy had a partial replacement of his left knee in 2011 at St. Vincent's Hospital, a tornado hit sections of Birmingham. Patients' beds were moved to the halls until the danger passed. For rehab Roy wore a gross, old pair of tennis shoes and I protested.

"Nobody will notice," he said. "Stop being so negative."

While he was working out I heard this exchange between him and the therapist. "Those are sure interesting tennis shoes. I don't think I've ever seen any like them. How old are they?"

"Oh, I've had them a while."

"They say Rod Laver under the Adidas logo. I don't recognize the name. He must have been before my time."

"He was one of the greatest tennis players of the 20th century. He played in the 60's."

"You mean 50 years ago? Those shoes are antiques!"

I should say. And he thinks no one notices what you wear.

Some view retirement like my cousin, Mickey Guice. When asked how he was doing he said, "I'm doing what I do best - nothing. I go to bed when I want to and I get up when I want. My biggest decision is where I will eat lunch."

Roy decided to go back to work in 2012 after 10 years of retirement. He was hired to do histories and physicals on medicare patients with either Blue Cross or Viva insurance. He was to determine if their diagnosis and if their medicines were correct. When he got through with the medical forms, he would ask permission to ask them two personal questions. If they agreed and then gave a works answer to the second question, Roy would ask permission to tell them what the Bible teaches about how to have eternal life in heaven. Then, he presented the gospel.

On the first day his first patient cried tears of joy when he accepted Christ. Another one also prayed that day. On the second day three prayed and on the third day four more.

Some days no one would pray but on others one or two or even three or four were added to the kingdom. On October 31 seven people were part of the 15 that prayed that week.

Of course, not all believed that you don't have to work your way to heaven. Those were some of the ones that called to complain to the company. Roy received an email from his employer that some people were expressing concerns over his religious views.

The next company email said, "We've had a few more calls about your discussing religion. Please don't discuss that with any more members."

Roy sent this answer: "Studies (American College of Physicians Internist, Vol. 32, No. 9, pg. 10) have shown that 50 to 90 percent of patients (depending on the setting) want physicians to address their spiritual needs and addressing their needs has become an important marker of clinical competency."

He went on to say, "If one asks permission from the patient to discuss spiritual issues and permission is granted, what is there to complain about? A patient may disagree with what is said but permission has been given to say it. Complaint calls are justified only if permission is not granted and the discussion ensues.

"I would never discuss any spiritual topic unless the patient gave me permission to do so. To deny patients dying of cancer, those in physical or emotional pain and numerous other medical problems, the right to discuss spiritual issues displays a lack of concern and empathy by the doctor regarding a topic the majority of patients need and wish to hear. This is clearly documented in the medical literature."

The supervisor's answer to this was: "We've had five complaints in the last three weeks that your actions weren't welcome. Make sure the members give their permission."

After being off the week of Thanksgiving, Roy had nine pray the next week.

Roy not only visited clients in the Birmingham area but also in a 60 mile radius. Many lived on unmarked county roads so Roy would spend hours trying to find their homes.

About 135 prayed before Roy gave up this job and went to work for the Birmingham Water Works.

The former black, female doctor was fired before Roy took that job. The majority of the employees were black and wanted another black physician hired. So even though the Water Works clinic was free, most boycotted it. This reverse discrimination caused Roy to quit because he was seeing so few patients.

Misunderstanding about prejudice can occur.

My daughter-in-law, Hope, and a friend went shopping for a boy's belt in a department store.

"We want to get a white boy's belt."

"What did you say?" the black sales clerk asked. He wasn't smiling.

"We need a white boy's belt."

"Could you explain what you mean by that."

"I mean ... could ... we ... get ... a ... white ... boy's ... belt."

When he made a noise in his throat, they decided to shop elsewhere.

As they walked away Hope finally saw the problem. "He thought we wanted a white boy's belt."

"We do."

"Yeah, but we should have said, 'We want a boy's white belt.'"

Roy's next job was Medical Director at Donaldson Prison. At a Bible study, while he was considering that position, he heard the verses in Hebrews about remembering the prisoners as if you were in prison too. He felt this was a direct confirmation that he was to take this employment.

God made this certain by causing Roy to be challenged by the variety and complexity of the many interesting illnesses there and giving him a love for the people he works with and many of the prisoners.

He knew he couldn't think of himself as better than they were. One of the prisoners later told him, "You are the only doctor we've ever had that didn't act like he would rather be somewhere else."

The first year he was there the staff told him to be sure and wear a costume for Halloween. Everybody would be wearing one. I had the perfect one. He looked so cute wearing the big, orange pumpkin suit, that covered him from his shoulders to his knees.

He walked into the admitting area of the prison but the officers stopped him and told him he could not wear that into the prison. But they let him carry it inside. He stopped at a staff bathroom and put it back on so he'd be dressed for the party before he went to the infirmary. They were teasing him. No one else was wearing a costume.

The most pain Roy ever had was the result of a herniated disc in his lower spine.

It was two weeks of agony while different treatments were tried but nothing relieved the pain. He had back surgery which stopped the leg and back pain but brought on other pain as a result of the operation. Only after three months did he experience relief. But like a leak in an old plumbing system, when you plug one place it just starts a leak somewhere else. Then Roy's 'repaired' knee became swollen and painful.

I had a second fall at home when I thought I was on the bottom step, but I wasn't. I fell and hit my face on the chest at the bottom of the stairs. It hurt so bad I couldn't move. Just then, Roy came in from work and saw me lying on the floor.

"Get up, Jo Anne. You've got to carry me to the emergency room. I've got a kidney infection. I am so sick. I'm having chills and fever. They may want to admit me."

I got up and packed a bag for him. Then, I drove him to UAB Emergency Room, letting him out at the door while I parked the car.

I was sitting in a chair in the cubicle with Roy when the doctor entered, looked at both of us and said, "Now, which one of you is the emergency?"

It had been about 30 minutes since I had hit my face in the fall and now bruises and a black eye had developed. Roy looked at me and said, "What happened to you?"

"I fell down the steps and hit my head on the chest at the bottom. That's why I was lying on the floor."

"Oh, I thought you were resting."

I didn't say anything but I don't remember resting on the floor ever and certainly not recently, since at my age I have trouble getting up from there.

The Tuesday Morning store was packed with women cramming the aisles at the after Thanksgiving sale. I was early to be sure and get the advertised nut cracker Christmas ornaments to give our daughter.

I quickly found several I thought she didn't have. Then, I squeezed by people still making their selections and got into the already long check-out line. Immediately in front of me was a 250 pound woman clutching a large, nondescript, black purse. In the other hand she held a package of holiday paper napkins, which she placed on the counter, paid for and then headed for the door.

Now, it was my turn. "Hello." I spoke to the checker as she scanned my purchases.

Suddenly, the door alarm sounded.

"Stop! Let me see in your purse," the store employee, checking me out, yelled at the woman who had been in front of me and was now about to exit the store.

"Are you talking to me?" the woman by the door innocently asked.

"Yes. Come here. I want to see in your purse."

Reluctantly, the woman walked over to the counter and opened her purse. Inside was an expensive, percale king-size sheet set. I saw that it had a thread count of 350 and was 100% Egyptian cotton.

"Oh, I meant to get those. I put them in my purse so I wouldn't forget."

"Then, I guess you are buying them."

"... Well, I don't know ..."

"You will buy them or go to jail."

With that alternative the woman pulled out her credit card, the sheets were scanned and she signed for the purchase. With receipt in hand she went out the door, got into her car and drove off.

I turned to the cashier. "Well, that was something. I was scared she might have a gun in her purse. How much do I owe you for my purchases?"

"Nothing."

"Huh?"

"The shop lifter paid for them."

"What ... how?"

"I had scanned your purchases but in the excitement I forgot. So when I rang up the sheets I didn't realize that it continued on your ticket. So she paid for your things too. Merry Christmas."

One evening an old Cherokee told his grandson about a battle that goes on inside of people. He said, "My son, the battle is between two wolves inside us all. One is evil. It is anger, envy, jealousy, sorrow, regret, greed, arrogance, self-pity, guilt, resentment, inferiority, lies, false pride, superiority and ego. The other is good. It is joy, peace, love, hope, serenity, humility, kindness, benevolence, empathy, generosity, truth, compassion and faith."

The grandson thought about it for a minute and then asked his grandfather, "Which wolf wins?"

The old Cherokee simply replied, "The one you feed."

A similar story to this American Indian legend was related by Billy Graham in his 1978 book, "The Holy Spirit: Activating God's Power In Your Life."

Both are saying that the battle is in the mind. What we believe determines our life, our actions and our fate. What we put in is critical. Put in trash, out come trash.

Put in drugs out come confusion and mental illness. Put in truth, out comes peace, regardless of the circumstances - not perfectly but always improving. God works in our heart to make this possible.

Chapter 25

OF ALL THE things I've remembered and told about Roy and his antics, I really topped them all.

It began innocently. I decided to go with church members to Lancaster, PA for a combination work and tourist trip. I didn't want to fly so I was thrilled when I learned that another lady, Vangie Thames, was driving and I could ride with her. We met at the church and loaded my suitcase and bags into her trunk. I kissed Roy good by and we were off to drive 833 miles in two days.

About 70 miles later I wanted to take a photograph. My camera was in my purse. It wasn't in the back seat so we stopped to get it out of the trunk. But my purse wasn't there either. Yes, it was still in floor of the passenger side of Roy's car back in Birmingham. Now, I had no money, no credit cards and no checks. It was too far to go back for it. Roy had to Fed-Ex it to me. You would never believe the cost - $90. So my mess up was worse and more expensive than anything he ever did.

But I wasn't sorry I went. The most significant thing a Christian can do for others is to present the gospel. The second most important is to help those people who do share their faith.

One of the ways to help them is through GAIN, the Global Aid Network, the humanitarian arm of Campus Crusade for Christ. It helps provide basic needs to refugees and people in the poorest regions, including those in the Middle East, Africa and even closed countries like Iraq, Somalia and North Korea. Many people in those areas have been told not to trust Christians. But if you bring food to the starving it provides a bridge of friendship to those who wouldn't otherwise hear the gospel. Actions brings results. Through the love shown to these people, they are frequently open to receiving the best gift of all when they hear the gospel.

GAIN can go to tough areas because they know the safest place in the world is in God's will.

"If I avoid risks and don't go where He tells me, I'm in far more danger by being disobedient to the King of Kings," said Al Goff, CEO and president of GAIN. "Jesus wants us to talk to them. Too many people worry about risks but when you are in the will of God you are fire proof."

Caroline Price remember when her husband faced surgery and she searched scripture to try to find help for her fear of possibly losing her husband, their business, their home and having to take their children out of Briarwood school.

"Verses just jumped out at me and assured me that God would take care of me and the children, even if Bill died."

Bill recovered completely and lived many more years.

At the Lancaster Distribution Center for GAIN 2,679 volunteers helped the mission by packing food, seed, clothes, quilts and other needed items to be shipped to areas where they are distributed by the Campus Crusade Staff, local pastors and friends.

Twenty-one members from Briarwood, including four teenage grandchildren, attended the summer 2016 session. Because it is so meaningful and enjoyable many of those have attended before. It's not all work. Briarwood Church's coordinator, Doral Elliott, arranged for for us to attend the Sight and Sound musical, Samson, to have dinner in an Amish home, to visit to a full size tabernacle reproduction, and to tour an Amish farm and the Amish countryside.

Children helping with this work develop a heart for the less fortunate and for the gospel. A nearby church brought 37 first through fourth graders to work during their summer camp program. Two of the favorite jobs for younger children are stringing beads to make gospel bracelets and assembling school supplies.

The four primary areas of pressing needs are providing clean water, food, health and care.

The shortages of safe, clean water and sanitation programs are the main sources of suffering and disease on earth. Even when water is available it is often contaminated, leading to illness. The biggest contaminator of water is human waste.

"It is better to provide clean water than trying to purify it with water filters." Goff said. "A septic tank for a school will clean the water for a whole village. A water borne disease, diarrhea, kills more children than Aids, Malaria, Tuberculosis or war combined. Water is the number one need for people."

Volunteers going overseas help community leaders get and maintain clean water and sanitation programs by drilling and maintaining wells, distributing filters and rain catchments and constructing latrines and toilets.

The second greatest need is food. According to the United Nations 6.5 million kids under the age of five die of hunger each year. Lack of food is due to to human violence, natural disasters and inequitable distribution of resources. With donations from companies and individuals GAIN provides meals for refuges and for areas with a hunger crisis. At the distribution center in just five days 42,336 meals of rice and lentils or beans were packed and shipped from the Lancaster operation.

For the people not displaced, seeds are sent for long term food security. On site farming techniques, such as drip irrigation and using compost, are taught.

On World Refugee Day that year 65.3 million people were

displaced from their homes - more than at any time in recorded history - most being from Syria and Iraq. This flood of refugees were chased from their homes and stripped of anything of value. Beside food they are given survival kits including blankets, clothing, shoes, items for shelter and school supplies.

Health is the third greatest need. While healthcare workers go on short term mission trips, volunteers help by refurbishing wheelchairs, walkers and crutches. Gain gives disposable medical supplies, medical equipment, vitamins, and hygiene kits. All this is used to introduce them to the Great Physician.

Care, the fourth need addressed, includes packing and sending new and used clothes, shoes and blankets for beds and wheelchairs.

One of the unique items made at the Logistics Center are washable, reusable feminine pads for women in poorer areas of the world without access to disposable pads. These were designed by Dana Cassell who recognized this problem on a mission trip to Zimbabwe. There women couldn't appear in public and girls couldn't go to school during their period, resulting sometime in their dropping out of school. She fabricated these pads of two pieces of flannel with a towel inset and a cloth cover. The pattern is traced on all layers, cut out and then sown together.

When supplied to a women's prison, where they had no feminine pads before, 90% of the women became believers.

What can you do to help?

"Pray, give, go or volunteer," said Goff. "Pray for those who will go to bed hungry tonight. Give to release suffering and restore dignity. Join the 12,000 who go on mission trips. Or volunteer at the Logistics Center in Lancaster."

A sign as you exit the building sums up the reason for volunteering: "One's life will soon be past. Only what's done for Christ will last."

I hobbled around all during the trip due to leg pain. When I got home Roy examined it.

"Go to the Emergency Room about 7 a.m. tomorrow and take a

book and a banana." he told me. He wrote down three possibilities for them to consider. After five and a half hours, the results of an ultra sound showed a blood clot in the calf of my leg.

For the rest of my life I'll have a danger of developing other blood clots. When riding I must stop every two hours and walk for 10 minutes. So I'll have to go by train or Roy will have to drive me. Even with those results I'm glad I went. God is not through with me yet. He could have cause that blood clot to go to my lung and taken me home but that wasn't his plan.

Once I knew just what Roy needed. He told me, as he watched from the choir, he saw me "waddle down the aisle". Waddle! I told him I'd be sure he wouldn't see that again. The next week while standing at the back of the auditorium, I waved at him in the choir to be sure I had his attention and then I skipped down the aisle to our usual pew about half way down. It got his attention and everyone else's to see an old, overweight woman skipping in church. There's a lot of advantages to being on time for early church.

I was a part of the ministry that delivers flowers to Briarwood church members and relatives who lived in nursing homes. At first I visited former Briarwood members at Somerby at St. Vincent's in Shelby County, at St. Martin's in the Pines in Irondale, AL and at Rittenhouse Senior Living in Hoover, AL, driving 50 miles round trip.

I needed a carrier with wheels for the many vases of flowers. I didn't remember having one but I found just what I needed in our playroom. The escalating handle could be raised to pull the carrier holding the vases. All the walking was tiring but I loved talking to friends I made there. If my legs were as strong as my tongue I could run races. Later with deaths and moves I was down to visiting only three people.

I knew it was time to stop when I lost my car. I had ridden that day with another couple, Lester and Sharon Mason, who were planning to start delivering flowers. We met at the first retirement home and went in their car. When we finished back at the church, we rode around the parking lots searching for my car.

"It wasn't stolen," I told them, "who'd want a dirty, 16 year old Ford with a cracked windshield and a missing hub cap."

Then I remembered it was at the nursing home. They drove me over to get it and followed me back to the church. I got my flower carrier out of their trunk, put it in my car and waved good-bye. But on getting out the carrier I left my keys in their trunk. Now they were gone. In the church membership office I looked up their number and tried to call but their mailbox was full. I felt like crawling in a hole. But the Lord answered my prayer and had the Masons discover my keys and bring them to me.

God has always looked out for me. In our early years a Jehovah's Witnesses couple began coming to our house to teach us about the Bible. After several weeks I asked them to stop coming. I was hungry for Bible knowledge but God put a fear in my heart about what they were teaching so we wouldn't be deceived into believing false doctrine and joining a cult.

Frank Barker's parents had prayed for him since he was a teenager. They didn't know, as treasurer of his high school fraternity, he had stolen some of the fraternity's money. He still thought he was a Christian in spite of that and other actions. Later in seminary he found out he didn't really understand the gospel.

God saved him physically several time and he felt led to become a minister. But while pastoring a small Alabama church, he wondered what does it mean to believe? From a little booklet of the same title he learned he wasn't a Christian when it explained you must trust Jesus to save you while not trusting in anything you have done. He trusted in that free gift of eternal life. That began his life-long, diligent ministry of sharing the gospel when ever possible, his love of God's word and his commitment to prayer.

Called to be the pastor of newly formed Briarwood Presbyterian Church for the summer, he remained as the pastor almost 40 years. His aim was to teach the Bible so his congregation could learn how to abide in Christ by being grounded in the Word. After his retirement from the pulpit, he continued serving the congregation in other ways, as pastor emeritus.

Harry Reeder lied that he was a Christian when he met Cindy because she would only date Christians. They were married six months later. When he quit attending church, Cindy quit too because she wouldn't go alone. But the Lord was continuing to work on Harry. He found a small Presbyterian church in Charlotte, NC where everyone used their Bible to follow along, as the gospel was given and explained. Cindy was glad to go even though she had been raised Baptist.

Because the church was small and Harry had been an athlete they were asked to work with the youth group. As the couple began working in that area of ministry God was working on Harry's heart as he began studying and teaching from the word.

On Christmas Day 1969 the wife of an elder in that church had a cerebral hemorrhage and died. Jimmy Elliot and his wife, Imogene, had four girls from five to 17 years old. The girls were asking for the Reeders to come and be with them when their mother died.

Observing Jimmy's steadfast faith, Harry heard him say, "I've loved Imogene very much, since we were young. But I would not have her back. She is much happier and in a better place, Heaven."

Harry was overwhelmed and later cried out to God, "Lord, if that is what it means to be a Christian, I want to be one too. Please forgive me. I trust your Son, Jesus. I promise I will do whatever you want me to do with my life."

From then on Harry had a persistent call to go into the pastoral ministry. Within a year he surrendered his whole life to study and preach the Word of God, which he has done ever since.

Years later when he gave his testimony one of the four daughters of Jimmy Elliot was sitting in the congregation. After the service she told Pastor Reeder, "Now after hearing you, I can have peace because I know God used my mother's death to cause you to spread the gospel by becoming a minister and that's how He is using you."

He has been Briarwood's minister since Frank Barker retired in 1999.

Chapter 26

GOD'S ULTIMATE GIFT is his payment for our sins. This brings a domino effect - a new heart to replace the stony one, a new nature with guidance from the Holy Spirit, a new family with God as the adopted father, the new gift of eternal life and a new home in heaven.

Over fifty years ago he gave me another gift - someone to love. What a gift! I'd asked for it for years. God was waiting for me to mature. He knew that marriage and motherhood would be the crucible to bring me to Him.

I didn't have the Holy Spirit so He sent Roy to correct and change me. His actions showed me how to behave. No respecter of status, he treats everyone the same. He studies God's word to allow the Holy Spirit to change him. And he serves Him by presenting the gospel to the lost, bringing many into His kingdom.

I didn't liked it when Roy told me I was wrong. But I needed correction about gossip, being submissive, getting even, not forgiving and bad mouthing others. I thank God everyday for Roy.

Roy thought he couldn't have children but God answered my prayer with three. The Lord allowed our first son to survive hanging in his mesh sided playpen when he was two months old. The second son as a toddler barely missed being hit by a car when he ran into the street from between two parked cars. Later both sons survived major auto accidents.

God answered prayers about mental illness, my migraines, and my daughter-in-law's breast cancer. He protected our granddaughter,

Julia, when she had a quarter partially blocking her airway and He restored Randy's pulse so he didn't lose his arm.

I wanted Roy to meet my needs without me telling him. As the source of my happiness, I felt devastated if he failed to think of me. After 53 years of marriage I see that your husband can never meet all your needs. Man wasn't designed that way.

God has to be the ultimate source of our contentment and joy whether we are married or single. Every person at some point will let you down, but the Lord will not.

I went to church to see if I would get to see my father again after his death, to get help raising the children and to know if the Bible was true.

Like a lot of other people, I often felt I was right even if I didn't have all the facts. This is especially true about Christianity. Some can think they know all about the Bible when they have never read it all the way through - even one time. That would be like me trying to treat your medical condition based on partial reading of a First Aid Manuel.

I was angry for years about that woman embarrassing me when I gave the wrong answer about how to get to heaven. If I hadn't been called on and embarrassed I would not have paid attention. But it made me determined to see if that woman was right or if I was right when I quoted my one Bible verse, "Faith without works is dead."

Susan Huff's phone call on the day I was going to commit suicide and the newsletter from God convinced me that God is real and that He loves me. The watershed event of my life was when I asked Christ to come into my life as Savior and Lord. Everything else that happened to me pales in comparison.

That's when I got the free ticket to heaven by believing that Christ's death and resurrection paid entirely for my sins, giving me the sin-free record necessary to be saved. I can't do anything to add to that. But I certainly didn't remain sinless because I sometime reverted back to my old nature. While that puts me out of fellowship with God, it doesn't destroy my relationship with Him as His forgiven child. He has forgiven all my sins, past, present and future. It's hard to confess sins, to admit what my loving Father already knows, but it is necessary.

I need Him to control me. Everyone wants fire insurance but most people don't want a boss. I didn't. Yet that is the other essential part of salvation. I had to submit to His being my Lord and ruling over my life. Daily and throughout life I had to learn to ask what Jesus wanted me to do.

The wonder of wonders is that God doesn't give up on His people. We can sin and even seem to fall away. But He is always there, ready for us to return to Him. He will never lose a single one who truly comes to Him.

When I had asked the minister about Jesus he gave me a book to read with the four gospels combined into one story. But I needed to be told what it means to believe in Jesus. That event demonstrated that everyone needs to be trained to share the gospel.

I was so shy I always had trouble talking to people. I felt I had nothing to say that they would want to hear. Now, I have the most important message. I love telling what Jesus's death and resurrection mean and inviting others to accept Him as Savior and Lord. The decision is not up to me. The Holy Spirit convicts. I'm just a plug - the power is the Holy Spirit.

Until you have experienced it, you can't imagine the joy of seeing someone respond to the good news. There is nothing as thrilling. Initially, sharing was not easy. It was scary but that must not keep you from obeying God. You'll make mistakes but it is o.k. You will get better with practice, as you do with any activity. Don't just learn how to share your faith but be committed to doing it. Prospects may reject salvation but they are rejecting the offer, not you.

Jesus began his ministry by telling His first disciples to become fishers of men and His last instruction was to "Go and make disciples of all nations ... teaching them to observe all that I have commanded you." At least twenty-four other verses also tell about the great commission. Remember we will be held accountable for not presenting the gospel to the lost.

Pastors Harry Reeder and Frank Barker both focus on evangelism as an important part of each believer's lifestyle.

God blessed my attempts by causing people to pray to receive Christ including my mother, my brother, our son-in-law, and two daughters-in-law along with other relatives, friends, acquaintances and even strangers.

As we began our marriage the dedication to marriage began to wane as the youth culture demanded free love in the late 60s and early 70s. Many believed that any form of perversion was acceptable. And getting out of marriage was no longer looked on as a tragedy and became guilt free with the new 'no fault' divorce laws. Results of families disintegrating were soaring numbers of divorces, illegitimate births and children living in single parent homes.[2]

Sexually transmitted diseases (STDs) rose because people became sexually active earlier and had more sex partners. Studies also indicated an increase due to association with drug use.[3]

"The most reliable method of avoiding STDs is to abstain from ... sex or be in a long term mutually monogamous relationship with a partner known to be uninfected," according to the Sexually Transmitted Disease Treatment Guidelines, 2015.[4] That is as God planned it from the beginning in faithful marriages.

Once syphilis was considered a pox due to the wrath of God and a punishment for immorality. As Christians we know all sin will be punished here on earth or after death if they are not covered by our accepting Christ's sin payment on the cross.

A new threat came on the scene when Acquired Immunodeficiency Syndrome (AIDS) was recognized in 1981. Caused by the Human Immunodeficiency Virus (HIV) it had killed an estimated 39 million worldwide by 2014.[5]

---

2   James Dobson, Focus on the Family Newsletter, May 1963, 4-5.
3   Dobson, 4-5.
4   "2015 STD Treatment Guidelines," Centers for Disease Control and Prevention, www.cdc.gov/std/treatment/
5   "Statistics: Worldwide," The Foundation for AIDS Research, July 2015, www.amfAR.org/worldwide-aids-stats/

Many of the common infections such as syphilis, gonorrhea and Chlamydia are treatable or curable but HIV/AIDS, Hepatitis B and Human Papilloma Virus (HPV) are treatable but not curable.[6]

The other demand of that pivotal time, but also another bad idea, was free drugs looked on as great recreation. Many entertainers came out in favor of legalized pot. Many of them died from drug overdoes or other drug related causes.[7] We didn't learn from the past. Now marijuana has been legalized in several states.

Doubt was cast on the existence of God which further loosened all restraints.[8] As stated in Judges 17:6 "Each man did what was right in his own eyes." Many today voice this same lie in the form of tolerance by saying what is right for Christians may not be right for people of other nations. The Christian worldview was being replaced by secular humanism with man as his final authority.

These are some of the false and dangerous practices that led up to where our society is today. Thankfully God prevented Roy and me from buying into those destructive patterns.

Certain events set the direction for my life. These were not coincidences but God instances. Looking back I see God's involvement when my life took some critical turn. Some were obvious. But others seemed so insignificant when they happened, I wasn't aware of His shaping my destiny.

My first memory, disobeying by eating salt, disclosed my lifelong tendency to defiantly sin and then want forgiveness but it also foreshadowed the role God would have in my life. Salt is used to preserve and to help in healing. So, salt is a symbol of God's work in every part of our lives as he seeks to prevent our rot from evil and as He heals us from our sins. God does that for all believers. Then, He wants us to be that salt - the salt of the earth to purify and preserve our culture.

God put the spiritual interest in my heart. As a young child I wanted to know why we attended church on Sunday, instead of Saturday

---

6   "The List of Curable and Incurable STDs," www.std.gov.org/stds/std.htm
7   Dobson, 3
8   Dobson, 4

as instructed in the Old Testament. A neighbor told me it was because we were celebrating Christ's resurrection, which took place on a Sunday and because that's when the early Christians met together.

Not planning to get an education, I only went to college to find a husband. I was looking for love. But God had plans for me to learn to write so I could tell others about Him and His involvement in our lives.

God showered unimaginable gifts on me from a TV show. I went to graduate school because I couldn't afford to work any more that year after all my winnings.

In my new job after graduate school I found evidence of staff practices that made it impossible to remain there. If I hadn't left that job, I wouldn't have been at the V.A. hospital to receive the answer to the greatest prayer request I ever made. Roy was the answer.

God has revealed himself to me through his word preached, taught, read as well as all these instances where He intervened for my benefit. But I am not the exception. God is at work in the life of every Christian.

Many interventions were answers to my prayers or the prayers of others. God answers all our prayers - yes or yes but wait for my timing or no I have something better planned for you. We may not know, until we get to heaven, how some of our prayers were answered.

I made my first list of our answered prayers for Roy's seventieth birthday party. I wanted our children, and especially our grandchildren, to see that you can rely on God. Make a list and you will be amazed how many and in what varied ways the Lord has acted in your life, like He did in ours.

My life story is riddled with examples of God at work. I got one of my best gifts late in life. When Mother moved in with us she wanted me to write her life story. I would question her and write down her answers. When I got a section written I would read to her what I had written. She'd make additions or corrections. After working on it almost daily for two years it was finished.

"It's not many people who get to live their life twice," she told me, "as I have in working on this book."

I was glad I did it for her, but I benefitted the most. Since childhood I wondered if my mother really loved me. It seemed I wasn't important to her; she was never available. The color of my hair and eyes were wrong.

Roy urged me to talk it over with Mother but I couldn't. She didn't know how her words had hurt me. It wasn't done intentionally and telling her couldn't change the past. It would only make her feel bad.

She had been hurt in her childhood. I knew she was ashamed of not having the right clothes to wear to school. And when they moved off the farm and came to Birmingham they saw how poor they really were.

As parents we pass down to our children what was passed down to us - at least to some extent. So I would have "caught" her feelings of inadequacy even without her saying anything.

As we were revising some pages about her childhood in her book she made the comment, "I was so ugly."

"Why do you say that, Mother? "You weren't ugly; you were beautiful."

"Oh, I always thought I wasn't pretty like my sisters. They got Mama's black hair and brown eyes. I had ugly dish-water blond hair when I was young. And I got washed out blue eyes. I wanted to look like Mama."

Tears filled my eyes as I realized she had been talking about herself all those years ago. She thought she was ugly, not me. If I was wrong about that, I could have been wrong in thinking she didn't care if her work kept her away from me. Now I saw she was trying to give us a better life.

Again, God had given me a great gift. My life of depression, of feeling I just didn't measure up, was based on a wrong assumption. So in my 60s I finally believed that my mother really did love me. I would never have known it if I hadn't written her story. Sometimes we must make ourselves do something we don't want to do and we are the one most blessed.

Throughout my life God has intervened for my protection and

growth. I'm thankful that He is active in his care of me. We all have trials. Our choice is how we respond.

Roy developed a fatal disease in 2017. His body is no longer making blood cells, which will eventually cause his death probably within five years. I asked Sandy Wheeler Brothers how she faced widowhood not once but two times.

"After the tears of that initial shock, I was thankful for each day I had with Louis Wheeler," she said. "Because he was a Christian I knew where he was going and leaned not to worry about tomorrow."

After he died Sandy wasn't looking for a new husband. She told herself that she wouldn't go out with anyone unless he came to her door bearing gifts.

Our church has a ministry to widows where they are visited by a deacon or elder to find what needs they have. When Sandy received that visit, there stood Glen Brothers bearing a fruit basket.

God had him show up with a gift just as Sandy had specified. They dated five years and were married almost two years before God called Glen home.

The scripture Sandy relied on during the loss of both her husbands was Psalms 118:24 NIV "This is the day the Lord has made; let us rejoice and be glad in it."

Thankful for another day she had with her husband, she didn't dwell on tomorrow. I determined to do the same.

Roy and I are both at peace. I don't want to lose him but we know where he is going, when he dies, so we choose not to be downcast. It's easy to say but hard to do. When we fret, we have to admit and confess it as a sin of disbelief and rebellion. God trains us to trust by slowly turning up the heat. We learn to trust God during the bad times, rarely during the good.

Whatever means the Lord uses we are to remember Him, our salvation and His promise of the world to come. Heaven is our home.

So I see God's actions in our lives are like footprints and fingerprints. Both are there whether we recognize them or not. We see the footprints - the times we can immediately see the evidences of God.

The fingerprints are there too, even if you don't see them at the time they are happening. You'll look back later and realize only God could have done that. Look for both signs of God in your life so you will be encouraged. Tell them to your family to help their faith. Recognizing His footprints and fingerprints helps you to concentrate on the important aspect of life, the spiritual, instead of the physical.

"... Do not forget the things your eyes have seen or let them slip from your heart as long as you live. Teach them to your children and to their children after them. ... so that they may learn to revere me." Deuteronomy 4:9 NIV. So we are to remember what the Lord has done for us and we are to be sure to pass them on to our children and grandchildren.

From childhood I was looking for love. I finally found out that I have the most important - God's. He loves you too. Make Him your life.

(I don't know where this goes:) All Bible quotations are from: The NIV Study Bible, 10th Anniversary Edition, copyright 1995 by the Zondervan Corporation, 1984)

(there are 64,514 words on 227 pages in 26 chapters)